Benchmark and Unit Tests

Grade 5

HOUGHTON MIFFLIN HARCOURT

Contents

Grade 5 Benchmark and Unit Tests

Name _____ Date _____

Reading and Analyzing Text

Read the article "House Made of Newspaper—Read All About It!" before answering Numbers 1 through 7.

House Made of Newspaper— Read All About It!

by Patricia Bridgman
photographs by Edna L. Beaudoin

From the street, this building in Pigeon Cove, Massachusetts, looks like a regular house or maybe a log cabin. The only hint that this house is *different* is the sign that says Paper House. Step onto the front porch and things really start to look odd. Those shiny, brown shingles have words on them. And pictures.

"Elis Stenman started building the Paper House in 1922," says the owner, Edna Beaudoin, who is Stenman's grandniece. "He was an engineer. He also loved newspapers. He read five of them every day."

Stenman thought it was wasteful to throw away old newspapers. (This was in the days before recycling centers.) Instead, he used them to build a vacation house in Pigeon Cove.

To start the project, Stenman "hired a carpenter to build wooden rafters, beams, and floors," Edna says. He also had electricity and running water installed in the house, but there was no heat and no bathroom. (The family used an outhouse; it was not made of paper, but the toilet paper, of course, was.) Edna says that after all this was completed, Stenman "sent the carpenter away and used paper for the rest."

Each shingle is made of carefully cut pieces of newspaper glued together with flour-and-water paste. The shingles have been varnished many times to keep out the wind, snow, and rain. The newspaper pieces are so discolored that they're hard to read at first. Stand close. Look hard. You'll see ads for flapper dresses, 150-dollar fur coats (which would cost several thousand dollars today), and 50-cent shirts.

1

The door is one of the few things here made of wood. Step through it and you'll see that the ceiling, walls, and furniture are made of newspaper. When the house was completed, in 1924, the Stenmans decided to fill it with paper furniture. This kept them busy for the next eighteen years.

"The furniture is made of little logs of rolled-up paper," Edna says, "but it is full-sized and as strong as wood furniture." The paper logs are 1/2 to 3/4 of an inch thick and generally three to ten inches long. To make them, "Mr. Stenman took a piece of wire, like a coat hanger, and bent it at one end to form a handle," Edna says. "He'd lay the wire across a strip of newspaper and turn the handle to roll the paper tight." If you've ever seen someone roll back the lid of a can of sardines, you'll understand how the log-maker worked.

Out of these paper logs, the Stenmans created paper chairs, a table, a bookcase, a cot, a settee, and covered a couple of working lamps. Even the fireplace is paper—on the outside. "The inside is brick," Edna points out, "so it's actually very safe." She keeps a fire extinguisher on hand, just in case.

The real piano that Edna used to bang away on as a child is covered with newspaper stories about Admiral Byrd's trips to the North and South Poles in

1926 and 1928. The grandfather clock is made of newspapers from the capitals of each of the forty-eight states. (This was in the 1930s—before Alaska and Hawaii became states.) The desk shows articles about Charles Lindbergh's flight across the Atlantic Ocean in 1927, and the cabinet that holds the old-time radio has stories about Herbert Hoover's run for president in 1928.

When all of the furniture was made, Elis's wife, Esther, made curtains from magazine covers as a finishing touch. She also rolled some strips of paper into colorful beads and folded others into German Christmas stars.

In all, over 100,000 newspapers went into the Paper House and its furniture. Still, millions of newspapers have been published since the Stenmans completed their project. Does Edna ever think about adding more newspapers to the house or papering her own house, which is just next door? Not really. She has enough work as it is, running the Paper House as a museum. And in her spare time, she has plenty to read.

Now answer Numbers 1 through 7 on your Answer Sheet. Base your answers on the article "House Made of Newspaper—Read All About It!"

1 Before explaining when, why, and how the Paper House was built, the author first

    A. describes how the Paper House looks from far away and up close.

    B. explains how Edna Beaudoin became the owner of the Paper House.

    C. gives directions on how to get to the Paper House in Pigeon Cove, Massachusetts.

    D. provides background on what happened to old newspapers before there was recycling.

2 Which words from the article tell about the first step Mr. Stenman took in building the Paper House?

    F. "He also had electricity and running water installed in the house. . . ."

    G. ". . . Stenman 'hired a carpenter to build wooden rafters, beams, and floors,'. . ."

    H. "Each shingle is made of carefully cut pieces of newspaper glued together with flour-and-water paste. . . ."

    I. ". . . the Stenmans created paper chairs, a table, a bookcase, a cot, a settee, and covered a couple of working lamps."

3 Read this sentence from the article.

> The newspaper pieces are so discolored that they're hard to read at first.

What does the word *discolored* mean in the sentence above?

A. colored again

B. altered in color

C. brightly colored

D. filled with color

4 Which of the following topics in the article does the author focus in on, using quotations and detailed descriptions?

F. how Mr. Stenman built the furniture

G. how Mrs. Stenman made decorations

H. why Mr. Stenman made the door out of wood

I. why Mr. Stenman built the house in Pigeon Cove

5 Read this sentence from the article.

> "The inside is brick," Edna points out, "so it's actually very safe."

If *actual* means "real," what does the word *actually* mean, as used in the sentence above?

A. not real

B. in reality

C. more than reality

D. becoming less real

6 Which step came last in the construction of the Paper House?

    F. The furniture was built.

    G. The fireplace was built.

    H. The curtains were hung.

    I. The shingles were varnished.

7 Before Elis Stenman could build the grandfather clock, he first had to

    A. read all the newspapers.

    B. make lamps in order to see.

    C. hire a carpenter to build the frame.

    D. collect a newspaper from each state capital.

Name _____ Date _____

Read the passage "Tamales Forever" before answering Numbers 8 through 13.

Tamales Forever

The summer I turned ten, my *abuelito* (grandpa), whom I had not seen since I was five, drove from Texas to visit us. That summer, all I wanted to do was ride my bike down to the creek to meet my friends. We found that the creek bed was a rough kind of clay, and we spent hours in the shade making small, though bad, sculptures of dogs, cats, snakes, and the like.

"Hola, nieto," Abuelito said, lifting me up for a bearish hug. *Nieto* meant grandson, and Abuelito was the only person who called me that.

"Hola, Abuelito!" I sang into his shirt, happy to find him exactly the way I remembered. He smelled of corn tortillas and hay, two smells of great goodness.

After he set me down, the grownups started talking, so I went outside. After a bit, I mounted my bike and raced off toward the creek. I arrived home in time for dinner, and in time to be greeted by my mother. Once she got me alone, she reprimanded me. She said I could not just chase around all day while my grandfather was visiting. I had to make sure to spend quality time with him.

"Doing what?" I asked. I couldn't imagine activities suitable for both of us.

"Be imaginative," my mother said, and waved her hand in the air as if I could just pull a rabbit out of a hat.

"Good morning, Abuelito," I said the next day when I bounded downstairs and found him working in the kitchen. "Are you making tamales?" He had a pile of corn husks spread out on the table next to a group of bowls holding water, black beans, a mountain of grated orange cheese, and yellow corn mush. I had seen my mother make tamales, and I hadn't paid much attention. A grandpa making tamales was more interesting. I wondered if I could make a sculpture with the mush.

"Nieto, why don't you try it yourself?" he said, patting the chair next to his.

At first I just watched him dip the corn husk into the water, lay it flat, slap some corn mush on top and mash it into a rectangle. Then, he made a thick line of beans along the mush and sprinkled cheese over them. Finally, he settled more mush over the beans and cheese and wrapped the husk around the tamale, tying it with a long shred of husk so it made a neat little package. I grabbed a corn husk and tried to do what he did, but my tamales were as sloppy as the clay sculptures I made at the creek.

When Mom came in from the store, she smiled at us. "Are we having tamales for lunch?"

I was surprised to hear that it was lunchtime already. I hadn't noticed the hours passing. "We're having tamales forever," I said.

Name _____ Date _____

After lunch, we took a *siesta* (nap) because we were too full to do anything else, but as soon as we got up, I asked Abuelito if he could ride a bike. My dad's was in the garage, and he wouldn't need it. He'd be at work until dinner anyway.

"Sí," Abuelito said, "I have a bike of my own at home, and I ride fast, faster than you, probably."

I raced Abuelito down to the creek to make sculptures of clay, which he was much better at than I or any of my friends were. He made a dragon, a lion, and a seal with a ball on its nose. The whole time my friends and I sat there watching, thrilled to see his fingers fly over the clay just like they had flown over his tamales.

Now answer Numbers 8 through 13 on your Answer Sheet. Base your answers on the passage "Tamales Forever."

8 The narrator's mother scolds him, because he has not

F. taken his nap.

G. cleaned off his bike.

H. finished making the tamales.

I. spent time with his grandfather.

9 Read this sentence from the passage.

I couldn't imagine activities suitable for both of us.

What is the meaning of the word *suitable* as it is used in the sentence above?

A. amusing

B. appropriate

C. normal

D. special

Name _____ Date _____

10 Read this sentence from the passage.

> "Be imaginative," my mother said, and waved her hand in the air as if I could just pull a rabbit out of a hat.

What does the phrase *pull a rabbit out of a hat* mean in the sentence above?

F. try out several different ideas

G. magically come up with an idea

H. get others to help decide on an idea

I. spend lots of time thinking of an idea

11 Which step in making tamales comes after making a thick line of beans along the mush?

A. dipping the corn husk into water

B. tying the husk around the tamale

C. sprinkling cheese over the beans

D. shaping the corn mush into a rectangle

12 During the visit, the narrator discovers that his grandfather

F. sells some of his art.

G. likes to nap after lunch.

H. is fun to spend time with.

I. wants to learn to ride a bike.

13 Which sentence best states the passage's theme or main idea?

A. A child acquires a new talent.

B. Abuelito learns to mold with clay.

C. A child learns to respect his elders.

D. Two relatives discover fun together.

Name _____ Date _____

Read the poem "Ducks" before answering Numbers 14 through 19.

Ducks

Those Spring-y ducks, those April ducks!
They puddle 'round and double up.
Two by two, and upside down,
they supper up,
those downside up and daft-y ducks!

Midsummer ducks, of plucky stuff,
their young quite buff in downy fluff,
move in a row like freeway trucks.
We never seem to see enough
of white, of yellow summer ducks!

October ducks! October ducks!
Weather cooling, feathers ruffed,
they gather strength, their chests are puffed,
and leave their puddle one chill day.
October ducks! Come back by May!

Winter passes, dark and duckless.
Bundled up, we skate the pond,
and wonder why we're so duck-fond.
Could be their quacks, their webby feet,
the waddling[1] way they like to greet.

---

[1] **waddling:** to walk with short steps from side to side

Name _____ Date _____

Now answer Numbers 14 through 19 on your Answer Sheet. Base your answers on the poem "Ducks."

14 Read these lines from the poem.

> **Those Spring-y ducks, those April ducks! / They puddle 'round and double up.**

What effect does the author's use of informal language in the lines above create in the poem?

F. It makes the ducks seem more realistic.

G. It gives the poem a light-hearted sound.

H. It helps readers better imagine the ducks.

I. It makes the speaker seem more trustworthy.

15 Read these lines from the poem.

> **Midsummer ducks, of plucky stuff, / their young quite buff in downy fluff, / move in a row like freeway trucks.**

What does the word *downy* mean in the sentence above?

A. shiny

B. spotted

C. soft

D. thick

16 Based on the way the speaker of the poem describes ducks, the reader can tell that the speaker

F. enjoys watching ducks.

G. is one of the younger ducks.

H. wishes he or she could be a duck.

I. only sees ducks during the summer.

17 Compared to the other three seasons, in winter

A. ducklings are born.

B. ducks swim single file.

C. ducks go underneath the water.

D. no ducks can be seen on the pond.

18 Each of the four stanzas in the poem

F. explains one interesting behavior of ducks.

G. explains what happens in a particular stage of a duck's life.

H. describes what the speaker observes about ducks during a season.

I. describes how the speaker's attitude toward ducks changes on different occasions.

19 Which of the following best tells the poem's theme?

A. Nature is constantly changing.

B. Animals and nature should be respected.

C. Some animals are meant to live in the wild.

D. People often have fondness for certain animals.

Read the passage "The Soccer Game" before answering Numbers 20 through 24.

The Soccer Game

by Chris Berriman
illustrated by Kathryn Mitter

"Go, Amanda, go!" Laura shouted as she watched her younger sister work the soccer ball toward the goal.

The ball rolled in front of Amanda's neat, controlled steps. Suddenly, *wham*, a player from the other team slammed into Amanda. In an instant, the ball was gone.

Laura's coach nodded. "Amanda's a good player," the coach said. "She's fast and sharp. Why don't you bring her to the next game? Maybe we can use her."

"Mandy doesn't think she's that good," Laura said. "She gets really upset when she loses."

After the game, Mandy sat by herself and removed her shin pads.

"Good game," Laura said. "You did a great job of handling the ball."

A red-faced Mandy muttered, "Thanks, but we didn't win." Not wanting to talk, she turned away to open her gym bag.

From across the field the coach hailed them. "See you Saturday, Laura! Remember to bring Mandy. And Mandy, bring your gear, too. You might see some action." Then she added, "Oh, and don't forget, Laura, we play the Rockettes. You know what that means." The coach smiled and waved goodbye.

Although at first Amanda was pleased and excited to be invited to play on the older girls' team, Laura noticed later that she was still upset. She sat down with Mandy in front of the television.

"What's on?" Laura asked.

Name _____ Date _____

"Some educational show about sailing ships or something," Mandy answered glumly.

"You still moping about the game?"

"It's always the same, Laura. I play my hardest and then some player elbows me and takes the ball when the ref's not looking. Maybe that's the way to win."

"No, it's not, and you know it," said Laura. Amanda just turned up the television.

". . . a famous battle between two fleets of sailing ships occurred in the 1500s," the television voice droned.

"Anyway," Laura spoke up to try to get over the sound of the television, where old sailing ships were getting set for a battle, "wait until you see the Rockettes. They're the biggest and toughest team in the league. We call them the Sock-ettes."

The television droned on. "The Spanish Armada had 130 of the biggest and most heavily armed ships ever assembled, but the smaller English ships were more maneuverable and were manned by skillful seamen."

"Hmm," said Amanda, slowly. "Is that so?" Laura wasn't sure if she was talking to her or not.

A week passed, and all too soon it was Saturday and time to face the Rockettes. It was a tough battle, and by the final minutes the score was tied 1-1. Amanda had dressed for the game but had not played at all. From the bench she gazed at the big Rockettes and the smaller players of her sister's team—and now her own—the Cleats.

"Wow," Amanda exclaimed, watching a Cleat player limp to the bench after a hard tackle. The coach turned and looked her over.

"All right, Mandy," the coach said, "there're only five minutes to go. Get ready. You're going in."

Soon Amanda was in the thick of the game, dodging and weaving between the much bigger Rockette players.

"Ah, here's a little one!" sneered a Rockette, moving in close to play defense.

Taking a pass, Amanda slipped away and dribbled nimbly down the sideline, the Rockette pursuing her. An even bigger Rockette made a beeline[1] toward her from the center of the field. At the last moment Amanda dodged, and the two Rockettes collided[2] behind her with a loud thud.

Stepping up her speed, Amanda suddenly faced two more Rockettes who seemed to loom over her like enormous warships.

"Man-oov-er!" she cried, and suddenly skipped the ball from one foot to the other. She pirouetted[3] around one player just as the other was about to hip tackle her to the ground, then dove right past the goalie and propelled the ball with a quick, sharp kick. The ball went straight into the net!

The crowd cheered and Mandy's new teammates grinned as they battled on defense as the last few seconds ticked off the clock. The game was over. The Cleats had won.

"Three cheers for the Rockettes," cried the Cleats.

"Three cheers for the Cleats," the Rockettes replied.

Laura wanted to add something.

"Three cheers for Amanda," she said, "who faced much bigger, stronger opponents and defeated them two ships at a time!"

Now answer Numbers 20 through 24 on your Answer Sheet. Base your answers on the passage "The Soccer Game."

20 Which of the following is the best description of the passage's setting?

   F. a time in the distant past

   G. a science-fiction future world

   H. a modern, realistic environment

   I. a fantasy place where anything can happen

---

[1] **beeline:** direct, straight line

[2] **collided:** to come together with forceful impact

[3] **pirouetted:** whirled about as in ballet

Name _____ Date _____

21 The Cleats players call the Rockette players "the Sock-ettes" because the Rockettes

    A. hit hard.

    B. like to win.

    C. wear socks.

    D. are all girls.

22 Amanda turns the TV volume up when Laura is trying to talk to her about soccer because

    F. Laura is giving Amanda bad advice.

    G. Amanda is avoiding Laura's questions.

    H. Amanda is interested in the TV program.

    I. Laura is trying to change to another program.

23 Read this sentence from the passage.

> **"The Spanish Armada had 130 of the biggest and most heavily armed ships ever assembled, but the smaller English ships were more maneuverable and were manned by skillful seamen."**

If *skill* means "talent," what does the word *skillful* mean in the sentence above?

    A. full of talent

    B. without talent

    C. increasing talent

    D. in a talented way

Name _____ Date _____

24 Read this sentence from the passage.

> "Man-oov-er!" she cried, and suddenly skipped the ball from one foot to the other.

Why does the author use the dialogue above in this particular scene from the passage?

F. to show that Mandy feels frustrated playing against the Rockette players

G. to show that Mandy is warning the Rockette players to get out of her way

H. to show that Mandy has figured out a strategy to get by the Rockette players

I. to show that Mandy has decided to play as roughly and aggressively as the Rockettes

Read the passage "Help Is Just a Click Away" before answering Numbers 25 through 29.

Help Is Just a Click Away

Rosa used the Internet to look up information for a report on deserts. While Rosa researched for her report, her mother watched the sites closely, ready to offer advice. When Rosa was finished, she had learned about deserts, but she had also learned what to look for in a website.

She began by typing the word *deserts* into a search engine. The search engine had over 8 million sites with something about deserts. This could take some time, thought Rosa.

Clues in the Address
Look for .com

First, she tried some of the sites with addresses ending in .com because that was what she saw most often. Many of these sites had good information, but much of it was for sale. She found links to specific books. Other links went to companies selling magazines and maps. She even found CDs that had songs with the word "desert" in the title. Interesting, but not helpful. She soon learned to be careful with addresses that ended with .com. This told her that a business or a person created the site. Sometimes, these sources were full of good, correct information, but other times, the people who made them just wanted to sell things. Also, the authors of these sites may have been experts on the subject. Others, it seemed, had created websites just for kicks.

Look for .gov

Some of the most useful information came from sites with addresses ending in .gov. These were government sites. USGS.gov was the website for the U.S. Geological Survey; it had maps and articles about everything Rosa could think of. It also let her click on any state to learn about deserts there. She could have gone to californiadesert. gov to study California's deserts. She learned about national parks located in or near deserts from nps.gov. This made Rosa want to visit a desert as a way of studying it.

Look for .org

Next, Rosa tried some sites with addresses that ended with .org. These were all organizations with connections to deserts. Some of these organizations, such as the National Geographic Society and the International Year of the Desert, had lots of information that seemed to be presented clearly and fairly. However, other organizations represented a single point of view regarding deserts, such as how to preserve desert habitat or change desert land into new neighborhoods.

Look for .edu

Finally, Rosa tried some addresses ending in .edu. These were from schools, colleges, and other educational groups. These were helpful because they were focused on presenting the information. Sometimes the sites were very specific, such as the one about the fleas found on a certain desert mouse. Another site had information about a proposed highway through a desert. Something helpful on that site was the date. The site had been written in 1992 and last changed, or updated, in 1994. By now, the building of the highway was history, not news.

Clues on the Site

As soon as she found a site, Rosa learned to look closely at the home page for clues about the author. She found better information when the home page named the person or organization responsible. People who took credit for their work appeared to be proud of it and seemed to make sure it was correct.

Links to the Author

She also looked for a link that said "About," where she learned about the site's authors. If the person taught about deserts at a college or had written books about deserts, she reasoned[1] that she had chosen a good site.

Lists of Sources

Some sites named the books or other sources that had been used to create the site. These sites told where all the words, ideas, photos, and other work on the site had come from. Lists of sources or other notes about the information showed the website author's concern for presenting correct information. This gave Rosa confidence in the accuracy[2] of her own report.

Other Clues

As her Internet study of deserts continued, Rosa found that she was asking the same questions with each new website. Are there links to other organizations or other useful sites? Do all the links work? Are all the words spelled correctly? Are there pop-up ads or things being sold? Using these clues helped Rosa find the most reliable Web sites.

Rosa worked hard to finish her report on deserts. She liked studying their climates and geography. Some day in the future, she may get to visit a desert and see firsthand the things she learned.

[1] **reasoned:** to conclude by logical thinking

[2] **accuracy:** correctness, free from error

Now answer Numbers 25 through 29 on your Answer Sheet. Base your answers on the passage "Help Is Just a Click Away."

25 Which of the following best describes how Rosa's role in the passage differs from her mother's role?

   A. Rosa is less interested in the Internet search than her mother.

   B. Rosa is less careful when doing the Internet search than her mother.

   C. Rosa is more knowledgeable about Internet searches than her mother.

   D. Rosa is more actively involved in the Internet search than her mother.

26 Readers are able to tell Rosa's thoughts in the passage, which helps readers better understand

   F. how the Internet has changed.

   G. the research process Rosa is using.

   H. the relationship between Rosa and her mother.

   I. why adult supervision is important when doing Internet research.

27 How did the sites that Rosa found with addresses ending in .com differ from some of the other sites she tried?

   A. These sites were often selling the information.

   B. These sites contained lots of maps and articles.

   C. These sites were created by government agencies.

   D. These sites often listed sources and notes about the information.

28 Read this sentence from the passage.

Others, it seemed, had created websites just for kicks.

What does the phrase *for kicks* mean in the sentence above?

F. for a friend

G. for practice

H. for enjoyment

I. for a challenge

29 Read this sentence from the passage.

These were all organizations with connections to deserts.

What does the word *organizations* mean in the sentence above?

A. governing bodies that create laws

B. the systems required to operate something

C. the buildings in which companies are located

D. groups of people working for a particular purpose

Name _____ Date _____

**Read the article "Dolores Huerta: Passion and Mission" before answering
Numbers 30 through 35.**

Dolores Huerta:
Passion and Mission

What motivates someone to travel far and risk arrest and danger just to help others?
In Dolores Huerta's case, it is a "sense of mission." From an early age, she says, "I
knew there was something I was meant to do."

Dolores Huerta was born in New Mexico in 1930, just as the U.S. entered the Great
Depression. Huerta's mother worked two jobs to make sure her children were provided
for. She insisted that each child help around the house. Her mother tried to help people
who struggled to find work and provide for their families. From her mother, Huerta
learned to work hard and help others. As an adult, Huerta was known as a symbol
for passionate commitment. It was because she put her whole heart into her efforts to
help others.

Huerta graduated from college and began to teach children in Stockton, California.
In fact, in Stockton there is a school named for her today. Many of her students were
poor children with parents who were farm workers barely making enough money
to survive. She knew they could not do their best to learn when they came to school
hungry, so Huerta decided that she could help her students best by helping their whole
families. Huerta had found her life's mission.

Huerta decided to help the farm workers bargain for better ways to work and live.
At this time, most farm workers in California worked long hours for low pay. The
work was hot and hard, and workers were often exposed to dangerous chemicals. They
sometimes had to pay for the water they drank at work. Many
farm workers did not speak enough English to talk with farm
owners about these and other problems.

Huerta first worked with the Community Service
Organization (CSO) to help make changes. She signed up
workers to vote and urged them to be active in the CSO. She
talked to governors and lawmakers about laws to protect farm
workers' health and pay. Then, with another activist named
César Chàvez, she cofounded what would become a new
organization, the United Farm Workers (UFW). Huerta and
Chàvez asked farm workers to join the UFW so they could help
them stand up for their rights.

Although the UFW went about its work in a nonviolent
way, sometimes crowds became angry and police were called
in. In 1988, while handing out information about workers'
problems, Huerta was hurt and had to go to the hospital, but

Name _____ Date _____

this experience did not stop her. Her courage drew notice and donations. Later, she was able to create the Dolores Huerta Foundation.

Huerta has retired from the UFW but still works for her foundation. Her mission today is the same as it was four decades ago: teach people they have a voice, and they can use it to make changes. Her passion and mission have inspired many.

Now answer Numbers 30 through 35 on your Answer Sheet. Base your answers on the article "Dolores Huerta: Passion and Mission."

30 According to the article, how did Huerta first learn about helping others?

    F. from watching her mother

    G. from helping out her siblings

    H. from her students in Stockton

    I. from living through the Great Depression

31 Read this excerpt from the article.

> **As an adult, Huerta was known as a symbol for passionate commitment.**

In the sentence above, the word *commitment* means

    A. dedication.

    B. fairness.

    C. trust.

    D. voice.

32 Which part of Huerta's life does the author focus most closely on?

    F. her support of farm workers

    G. her work with her foundation

    H. her experience in the hospital

    I. her school experiences as a child

33 Which organization did Huerta first work with to improve conditions for migrant workers?

    A. the school in Stockton

    B. the United Farm Workers

    C. the Dolores Huerta Foundation

    D. the Community Service Organization

34 Why does the author dedicate a paragraph to providing background information on the working conditions of California farm workers?

    F. to show how Huerta first met César Chàvez

    G. to show why Huerta wanted to become a teacher

    H. to show why Huerta wanted to work for farm workers' rights

    I. to show how Huerta went about influencing leaders to change laws

35 Read this sentence from the article.

> **Although the UFW went about its work in a nonviolent way, sometimes crowds became angry and police were called in.**

What does the word *nonviolent* mean in the sentence above?

    A. enjoyable

    B. harsh

    C. outspoken

    D. peaceful

Name _____ Date _____

Revising and Editing

Read the introduction and the passage "Something Unexpected" before answering Numbers 1 through 7.

Greg wrote this passage about something surprising that happened to him. Read his passage and think about the changes he should make.

Something Unexpected

(1) In many stories, the conclusion often turns out as you expect. (2) However, this happens less often in real life. (3) Recently, something in my life. (4) Had an unexpected ending.

(5) The situation began as follows. (6) We live next door to a sweet, elderly lady named Mrs. Keller. (7) My father noticed that Mrs. Keller had not been outside much lately, which was unusual because she loved working in her garden. (8) My mother also noticed that the plants in Mrs. Keller's yard were looking overgrown. (9) My parents were worried about her. (10) They went next door and found out that Mrs. Keller had been sick. (11) They decided that our family should offer Mrs. Keller our assistance. (12) We would spend a few hours the following weekend getting her yard back into shape.

(13) I wasn't eager to participate but I had no choice in the matter. (14) By nine o'clock in the morning, I was in Mrs. Keller's yard using the tools my father had

given to me to dig up weeds. (15) I had to dig carefully so I didn't disturb any of the flowers that Mrs. Keller had planted last spring.

(16) It was only noon, but it seemed like I'd been working for a very, really long time. (17) It was exhausting work, and I was getting tired and out of breathe. (18) Suddenly I heard a clinking sound as my shovel hit something hard. (19) I stopped working. (20) I picked up the object that the shovel had struck. (21) I was excited to discover it was a large arrowhead! (22) Later, Mrs. Keller told me that I could keep it as a souvenir, in appreciation for my assistances.

(23) I thought working in our neighbor's yard would be boring.

(24) Instead, I found an exciting piece of history. (25) I can't wait to help out next weekend and see what I discover next!

Now answer Numbers 1 through 7 on your Answer Sheet. Base your answers on the changes Greg should make.

1 What revision is needed in sentences 3 and 4?

A. Recently, something in my life had an unexpected ending.

B. Recently, something in my life, had an unexpected ending.

C. Recently, something. In my life had an unexpected ending.

D. Recently, something in my life that had an unexpected ending.

2 What is the best way to revise sentences 9 and 10?

   F. My parents were worried about her, later they went next door and found out that Mrs. Keller had been sick.

   G. My parents were worried about her, or they went next door and found out that Mrs. Keller had been sick.

   H. My parents were worried about her, so they went next door and found out that Mrs. Keller had been sick.

   I. My parents were worried about her, however they went next door and found out that Mrs. Keller had been sick.

3 What change should be made in sentence 13?

   A. change *eager* to *eeger*

   B. insert a comma after *participate*

   C. insert a comma after *choice*

   D. change the period to a question mark

4 What change should be made in sentence 16?

   F. change *was* to **were**

   G. change *seemed* to **seems**

   H. change *I'd* to **I'm**

   I. change *for a very, really long time* to **for ages**

5 What change should be made in sentence 17?

   A. change *exhausting* to **exhaust**

   B. insert a comma after *tired*

   C. change *out* to **outer**

   D. change *breathe* to **breath**

6 What is the best way to revise sentences 19 and 20?

    F. I stopped working and picked up the object that the shovel had struck.

    G. I stopped working and picking up the object that the shovel had struck.

    H. I stopped working and picked up. The object that the shovel had struck.

    I. I stopped, I stopped working, and I picked up the object that the shovel had struck.

7 What change should be made in sentence 22?

    A. change *me* to **I**

    B. change *keep* to **keeping**

    C. change *souvenir* to **suvenir**

    D. change *assistances* to **assistance**

Read the introduction and the passage "The Swimming Lesson" before answering Numbers 8 through 14.

Jasmine wrote this passage about a girl who wants to learn to swim. Read her passage and think about the changes she should make.

The Swimming Lesson

(1) Amelia sat on the edge of the community swimming pool, which is open to the public every summer. (2) A group of kids was swimming, or Amelia just stood at the edge of the pool near the lifeguard, watching sadly. (3) She wanted more than anything to join them, but she was very, really scared of the water. (4) Because of her fear, she had never learned how to swim. (5) Now she had to wait on the side of the pool while her family enjoyed themselves.

(6) The summer before, an older cousin had tried to teach Amelia how to swim. (7) He was confident that his swimming lessons would do the trick. (8) Amelia put forth her best effort but she could not control her fear. (9) She struggled with getting in the water so much that her cousin decided that he would never be able to teach Amelia. (10) That collection of memories were painful.

(11) Amelia was remembering those lessons when a girl sat down beside her. (12) The girl introduced herself, saying, "My name is Wendy. (13) Would you like to swim with me?"

(14) Amelia was a little embarrassed as she explained that she did not know how to swim.

(15) Wendy very smiling and said, "I know exactly how you feel. (16) In fact, until a few weeks ago, I wasn't able to swim either, if I can learn, you can definitely learn, too."

(17) With that, Wendy hopped in the water and held out her hand. (18) "If you'd like, I could demonstrate what I learned. (19) We could go out slowly, and we'll stop where the water reaches your middle."

(20) Amelia realiezed that if Wendy could conquer her fear, then maybe she could, too. (21) Carefully lowering herself into the pool, Amelia said to her new friend, "Maybe you can start by showing me how to move my arms, while I keep my feet on the ground."

Now answer Numbers 8 through 14 on your Answer Sheet. Base your answers on the changes Jasmine should make.

8 What is the best way to revise sentence 2?

   F. change *A* to **The**

   G. delete the comma after *swimming*

   H. change *or* to **but**

   I. change *watching* to **watched**

9 What is the best way to revise sentence 3?

   A. change *anything* to **any thing**

   B. change *them* to **they**

   C. change *very, really scared* to **afraid**

   D. insert a comma after *scared*

10 What change should be made in sentence 8?

   F. change *put* to **puts**

   G. change *forth* to **fourth**

   H. insert **most** before *best*

   I. insert a comma after *effort*

Name _____ Date _____

11 What change should be made in sentence 10?

   A. change *That* to **A**

   B. change *collection* to **collect**

   C. change *were* to **was**

   D. change *painful* to **painfully**

12 What change should be made in sentence 15?

   F. change *very smiling* to **grinned**

   G. insert a comma after *and*

   H. change *exactly* to **exact**

   I. change *feel* to **feels**

13 What is the best way to revise sentence 16?

   A. In fact, until a few weeks ago, I wasn't able to swim either, or if I can learn, you can definitely learn, too."

   B. In fact, until a few weeks ago, I wasn't able to swim either, but if I can learn, you can definitely learn, too."

   C. In fact, until a few weeks ago, I wasn't able to swim either, then if I can learn, you can definitely learn, too."

   D. In fact, until a few weeks ago, I wasn't able to swim either, because if I can learn, you can definitely learn, too."

14 What change should be made in sentence 20?

   F. change *realiezed* to **realized**

   G. change *that* to **so**

   H. change *could* to **can**

   I. delete the comma after *fear*

30

Name _____ Date _____

Read the introduction and the passage "A Good Way to Earn Money" before answering Numbers 15 through 20.

Barry wrote this passage about how he earned money for a new soccer ball. Read his passage and think about the changes he should make.

A Good Way to Earn Money

(1) Like most people, I sometimes want to buy things for myself. (2) Of course, buying things requires money. (3) One way to earn money is by doing small jobs for people you know.

(4) Last summer, I really wanted to get a new soccer ball. (5) I discussed the idea of doing some small jobs with my parents and then they spoke with some of our neighbors and relatives. (6) I quickly found that there were many, very job possibilities. (7) Most of the people my parents spoke with. (8) Didn't have time to do all of their household chores or yard work. (9) This is where I came to the rescue. (10) I mowed lawns, weeded gardens, and painted fences. (11) I took care of pets.

(12) Before I started a new job, I found out how much the person would pay me. (13) I also found out how much time I had to do the work. (14) I wanted to accept every job. (15) I only took on those I knew I had time for. (16) Once I accepted a job, I worked hard and did my very best. (17) By the end of the summer, I had earned enough money to buy that soccer ball, as well as a set of paints for my little brother. (18) I also had some money to start a savings account.

(19) If you decide to earn money this way, try to do jobs that interest you and best utilize your skills and talents. (20) Then you'll be making money and enjoying yourself at the same time. (21) When you work hard and treat

Name _____ Date _____

everyone with respect, your list of satisfied customer grows. (22) Earning your

own money will be fun, and it is good experience for the future.

_____

**Now answer Numbers 15 through 20 on your Answer Sheet. Base your answers
on the changes Barry should make.**

15 What change should be made in sentence 5?

    A. change *they* to **them**

    B. insert a comma after *parents*

    C. change *then* to **than**

    D. insert a comma after *neighbors*

16 What change should be made in sentence 6?

    F. change *quickly* to **quicker**

    G. change *found* to **find**

    H. change *there* to **they're**

    I. change *many, very* to **dozens of**

17 What revision is needed in sentences 7 and 8?

    A. Most of the people. My parents spoke with didn't have time to do all of their
household chores or yard work.

    B. Most of the people my parents spoke with didn't have time to do all of their
household chores or yard work.

    C. Most of the people my parents spoke with they didn't have time to do all of
their household chores or yard work.

    D. Most of the people my parents spoke with, and they didn't have time to do
all of their household chores or yard work.

18 What is the best way to combine sentences 10 and 11?

 F. I mowed lawns, weeded gardens, painted fences, took care of pets.

 G. I mowed lawns, weeded gardens, painted fences, and took care of pets.

 H. Taking care of pets, I mowed lawns, weeded gardens, and painted fences.

 I. I mowed lawns, weeded gardens, and painted fences while taking care of pets.

19 What is the best way to combine sentences 14 and 15?

 A. I wanted to accept every job, I only took on those I knew I had time for.

 B. I wanted to accept every job, but I only took on those I knew I had time for.

 C. I wanted to accept every job also I only took on those I knew I had time for.

 D. I wanted to accept every job and then later I only took on those I knew I had time for.

20 What change should be made in sentence 21?

 F. change *and* to **a comma**

 G. change *treat* to **treet**

 H. change *grows* to **grow**

 I. change *customer* to **customers**

Writing to Narrate

Read the prompt and plan your response.

Most people want to make their school or community a better place.

Think about what a group of children might do to make their school or community a better place.

Now write a story about a group of children who do something to make their school or community a better place.

Planning Page

Use this space to make your notes before you begin writing. The writing on this page will NOT be scored.

_____

_____

_____

_____

_____

_____

_____

_____

_____

_____

_____

_____

Name _____ Date _____

Begin writing your response here. The writing on this page and the next page WILL be scored.

_____

_____

_____

_____

_____

_____

_____

_____

_____

_____

_____

_____

_____

_____

_____

_____

_____

_____

_____

_____

_____

_____

_____

_____

_____

_____

Name _____ Date _____

_____

_____

_____

_____

_____

_____

_____

_____

_____

_____

_____

_____

_____

_____

_____

_____

_____

_____

_____

_____

_____

_____

_____

Name _____ Date _____

Reading Complex Text

Read the passage "Kid of Many Hats." As you read, stop and answer each question.
Use evidence from the passage to support your answers.

Kid of Many Hats

From under the cover of my large cowboy hat, I scanned the faces of the growing crowd on the perimeter of the city plaza. Usually, I disliked the heavy felt sombrero hat that was part of my costume, but today I was grateful for it. The swooping brim was ideal for ducking under to hide. I breathed a sigh of relief. I hadn't spotted any of my classmates in the crowd—yet. Tipping the brim of my hat down lower, I caught my sister Lupita's eye and grinned sheepishly. I could never fool Lupita.

Gathering her full white skirt woven with multi-colored ribbons, Lupita made her way to my side. "Don't worry, Javi. No one could possibly recognize you without your t-shirt and skateboarding shoes," she teased, gently tugging at the red tie on my three-piece suit.

1 How does Javi's point of view influence the way events are described in the section above?

_____

_____

_____

Lupita turned as a group of girls in the crowd shouted her name in chorus. I groaned, but Lupita waved excitedly at her seventh-grade friends who had come to watch. "You *want* your friends to watch?" I asked.

"Sure!" she responded brightly, adding, "But I didn't used to." I rolled my eyes, but I knew that Lupita understood.

It wasn't that I didn't like folk dancing. Folk dancing was deeply rooted in our Mexican tradition and culture. Every celebration, or *fiesta*—weddings, birthdays, holidays, even backyard picnics—involved dancing. It was a joke in our family that both Lupita's and my first steps as toddlers had actually been polka steps. For as long as I could remember, we'd been performing as part of our local *ballet folklórico*, or Mexican folk dancing, troupe. I was proud of being Mexican American, proud of my cultural heritage. It's just . . . with my friends at school, I talked about skateboarding and complained about math homework. My family, my community, and dancing—that was separate. And I liked it that way.

Name _____ Date _____

2 Tell how Javi and Lupita's feelings about folk dancing are alike and different.

_____

_____

_____

The sound of the audience clapping startled me back to the present. From her spot on the podium, the coordinator of this year's Hispanic Heritage Festival was beaming and gesturing in our direction. She had evidently just finished our troupe's introduction, which meant we were up next. The *mariachi* musicians launched into a lively tune: first the acoustic and bass guitars, and then the high-pitched five-string guitar and the violin. On cue, the girls floated out into the center of the plaza, their colorful skirts whirling like pinwheels. Lupita was always fun to watch. Her movements were fluid and graceful; what's more, she danced with her chin high and a broad smile on her face.

When the trumpets sounded, I joined the other young men in our troupe out on the plaza, our boot-heels stomping in rhythm to the music. With my left arm folded across my stomach and my right arm flung out to my side, I danced around my female partner, Amaya. As the music quickened, so did our feet. I had danced the *jarabe*, often called the Mexican Hat Dance, so many times that I didn't even have to think about the steps. When the dance finally ended, and the audience burst into raucous applause, I took a deep, breathless bow alongside my fellow troupe members. I had forgotten to care about who was in the audience. Lupita, her face flushed and happy, caught my eye. I grinned back at her, took off my sombrero, and tossed it high in the air.

3 How do the photographs contribute to the reader's understanding of the passage?

_____

_____

_____

After our performance, we all dispersed. Lupita ran toward her girlfriends, the other dancers to their family and friends. Just as I turned on my heel to go find my duffle bag, someone shouted, "Hey, Javi!" I recognized the voice of Norah, a girl in my class, behind me. Several other kids from Mr. Chow's fifth-grade class were with her. Part of me wanted to crawl in a hole and hide, but I turned on my boot heel to face my friends. So much for keeping dancing and school separate, I thought.

"We thought that was you!"

"That was so cool!"

"I didn't know you could dance like that! Where did you learn? You should teach us!"

I was speechless. As I struggled to respond to their onslaught of questions, Lupita suddenly appeared by my side. "Javi's just modest," she said. "You probably thought that all Javi could do was skateboard, but my brother is a kid of many hats. Dancing is just one of his many talents." She squeezed my shoulder, winked, and then floated, graceful as always, back to her friends.

Slowly, I let out a breath and laughed, "Of course I can teach you…"

4 How do Javi's friends react to his dancing? What lesson does this help him learn?

_____

_____

_____

_____

_____

Reading and Analyzing Text

Read the passage "Return of the Ridleys" before answering Numbers 1 through 18.

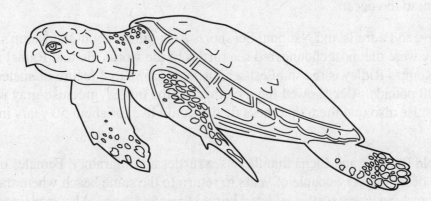

Return of the Ridleys

"Wow!" said Rafael, looking at the beach that stretched for miles. He and his sister stared out the windows of their older brother Alex's car. "I knew Hurricane Ike had caused a lot of damage, but I never dreamed the island would look like this."

The coastline of Padre Island National Seashore was dotted with trash, including milk cartons, sofa cushions, and even refrigerators. A seabird sat on a rocking chair, which was still in one piece. The chair looked as if someone had recently been sitting in it, looking out to sea. More trash floated on the water, waiting to wash onto the beach.

Rafael and Elena got out of the car. Elena stepped away from her door and looked at the ground. She had wanted to take her shoes off and feel the soft, warm sand on her bare toes. Instead, the ground was nothing but hard, clammy clay. She glanced at Alex. He was no longer animated and smiling as he had been in the car. The light had drained from his face. As he looked around him, his eyes widened and his mouth remained open, as if mid-sentence.

Alex got out of the car and looked at us "Well, there probably won't be any turtles nesting here for years. I'm not sure even the plan to restore the beaches will work, at least not in time. The turtle population was already threatened before the storm. The damage from the storm just adds insult to injury."

Alex was studying marine biology at the University of Texas in Austin. He had become interested in the ocean as a child, taking trips there with his family. Now his parents were letting him take his preteen brother and sister with him on a class assignment. He was doing a report on the sea turtles that nested on the Gulf Coast.

They all had heard of the serious storm on the Gulf Coast, but none of them had seen firsthand the problems that people faced in rebuilding after the storm. The sea-turtle facility in Galveston, Texas, had also been damaged by the hurricane. It was unlikely that it would be repaired in time to help the turtles during the upcoming nesting season.

Alex and his siblings had watched videos of sea turtles struggling onto sandy beaches. They had also watched videos of female turtles dragging themselves through the sand to find a nesting spot. The turtles used their flippers to dig holes where they would lay and bury their eggs. Elena and Rafael were amazed by the night photography that showed baby turtles racing out to the ocean.

On their drive to Padre Island National Seashore, Alex talked about the Kemp's Ridley sea turtles. They were the most endangered sea turtles in the world. He told Rafael and Elena that the Kemp's Ridley is the smallest sea turtle. It grows to 2 feet in diameter and weighs up to 100 pounds. Alex showed them pictures of the turtles' greenish-gray shells and light bellies. He also told them that these turtles could live for about 50 years in the wild.

Alex also told Raphael and Elena that these sea turtles are migratory. Females often swim hundreds of miles every couple of years to return to the same beach where they were hatched. Once on shore, these turtles laid and buried their own eggs. Alex explained that because only 1,000 female turtles are still known to exist, the future of these turtles is in question.

The three walked together down the beach, skirting the messes. "I wish we could pick it all up and haul it off," said Elena, "but there's just too much of it. Even if we worked all day, every day for a year, it wouldn't make a dent in this problem."

"True, but a journey of a thousand miles begins with a single step," replied Alex.

Rafael stopped suddenly and pointed. "What's that moving over there?" he asked. Three pairs of eyes searched the beach.

"I think it's a turtle!" exclaimed Alex. "Let's go see to make sure. We'll be able to get fairly close, but let's approach it carefully so it's not alarmed."

As they got closer, all three became more excited; they could tell it was a Kemp's Ridley! At least one turtle had returned safely, in spite of what it had gone through to get there. The three watched the turtle hunting for a sand dune. This single turtle's presence made them hopeful. Perhaps it was a good sign for turtles after all.

Now answer Numbers 1 through 18 on your Answer Sheet. Base your answers on the passage "Return of the Ridleys."

1 What surprises Rafael when he arrives on the island?

    A. the high winds of the hurricane

    B. the fact that the sand has changed to hard clay

    C. the amount of damage caused by the hurricane

    D. the large number of sea turtles that are on the beach

2 Read this sentence from the passage.

    A seabird sat on a rocking chair, which was still in one piece.

Which word sounds the same as the word *piece*?

    F. pace

    G. pass

    H. peace

    I. peas

3 Read this excerpt from the passage.

    The coastline of Padre Island National Seashore was dotted with trash, including milk cartons, sofa cushions, and even refrigerators. A seabird sat on a rocking chair, which was still in one piece. The chair looked as if someone had recently been sitting in it, looking out to sea.

The image described above best helps readers visualize

    A. how powerful and destructive the hurricane was.

    B. how the island's birds were affected by the hurricane.

    C. how few people have come to the island since the hurricane.

    D. where the hurricane began and ended, as well as the path it took.

4 Read this sentence from the passage.

> **Instead, the ground was nothing but hard, clammy clay.**

What does the word *clammy* mean in the sentence above?

F. dry and hot

G. damp and cool

H. rough and cold

I. muddy and warm

5 Read this excerpt from the passage.

> **The light had drained from his face. As he looked around him, his eyes widened and his mouth remained open, as if mid-sentence.**

In the excerpt above, readers can tell that Alex feels

A. shocked and sad.

B. annoyed and restless.

C. discouraged and angry.

D. excitement and dismay.

6 At the beginning of the passage, Alex is upset because he thinks

F. Rafael and Elena do not like the beach.

G. no one has made a plan to restore the beaches.

H. someone has left a rocking chair on the beach.

I. the turtles will not return to the beach for a long time.

Name _____ Date _____

7 Read this sentence from the passage.

> **He had become interested in the ocean as a child, taking trips there with his family.**

Which word has the same beginning syllable as the word *become*?

A. because

B. beckon

C. belly

D. benefit

8 Read this sentence from the passage.

> **Now his parents were letting him take his preteen brother and sister with him on a class assignment.**

What does the word *preteen* mean in the sentence above?

F. much smaller

G. more childish

H. younger than thirteen

I. nearly the same height

9 Read this excerpt from the passage.

> **Alex and his siblings had watched videos of sea turtles struggling onto sandy beaches. They had also watched videos of female turtles dragging themselves through the sand to find a nesting spot. The turtles used their flippers to dig holes where they would lay and bury their eggs.**

What can the reader conclude from the excerpt above?

A. There are lots of sea turtles in the world.

B. It is unusual to see sea turtles on the beach.

C. It is hard work for sea turtles to build a nest.

D. There are many dangers for baby sea turtles.

10 Read this sentence from the passage.

> **Elena and Rafael were amazed by the night photography that showed baby turtles racing out to the ocean.**

What does the word *photography* mean in the sentence above?

F. scientific studies

G. struggle for survival

H. research done outdoors

I. pictures taken with a camera

11 Read this sentence from the passage.

> **They were the most endangered sea turtles in the world.**

In the sentence above, the word *endangered* means

A. completely gone.

B. difficult to count.

C. in danger of disappearing.

D. dying of disease and hunger.

12 The reader can conclude from the passage that Alex

F. knows a lot about sea turtles.

G. has never been to the island before.

H. has lived on the coast all of his life.

I. has worked to help sea turtles in the past.

Name _____ Date _____

13 Read this sentence from the passage.

> "True, but a journey of a thousand miles begins with a single step," replied Alex.

What is meant by the adage *a journey of a thousand miles begins with a single step*?

A. Hard work always pays off in the end.

B. Some jobs are just not worth your time and energy.

C. No matter how difficult a task is, you must start somewhere.

D. There is a solution to every problem—you just have to find it.

14 What generalization can the reader make about sea turtles?

F. Sea turtles never return to a damaged beach.

G. Male sea turtles are good at taking care of their babies.

H. Baby sea turtles depend on their parents for a long time.

I. Female sea turtles always remember where they were born.

15 Read this sentence from the passage.

> We'll be able to get fairly close, but let's approach it carefully so it's not alarmed.

Which word has the same beginning syllable as the word *approach*?

A. action

B. admire

C. ahead

D. arrow

16 Read this sentence from the passage.

> **This single turtle's presence made them hopeful.**

What does the word *presence* mean in the sentence above?

F. manner or behavior

G. way of moving about

H. current existence in a place

I. response to an environment

17 Read this sentence from the passage.

> **This single turtle's presence made them hopeful.**

Which word has almost the same meaning as the word *hopeful* as it is used in the sentence above?

A. encouraged

B. grateful

C. joyful

D. lucky

18 Which word from the passage is a compound word?

F. approach

G. coastline

H. diameter

I. rebuilding

Read the articles "Arches National Park" and "Be a Park Volunteer" before answering Numbers 19 through 35.

Arches National Park

Arches National Park in Utah is one of America's most interesting parks. It is in a high desert and has elevations between 4,000 and 5,700 feet above sea level. The park has more than 2,000 naturally formed rock arches, which is more than any other place in the world.

Weather Shapes the Land

The rocks were shaped over time by wind, water, and ice. Thin sandstone walls resemble[1] the fins on a fish's back. Water seeps into cracks in the rock, breaking the rock into pieces when the water freezes. Huge pieces of stone give way as the air heats and cools when the seasons change. When a 3-foot opening appears, it is called an arch. Arches can be as wide as 300 feet.

Living in a Harsh Environment

The park has little rainfall. Its climate ranges from extremely hot summers to below-freezing winters. Animals and vegetation must struggle to survive there. Today, plants get help growing from a type of "living soil" that allows plant life to take root. The "living soil" is a knobby, black crust made of living organisms that spreads across the ground and holds loose soil together, preventing wind and water erosion. It also collects what little rain that falls and stores it for plants to use. Park signs warn people to avoid walking on this soil so they don't damage it.

Even though the park today looks much like it has for thousands of years, appearances can be deceiving. The park continues to change. Rock wears down; arches fall; new arches form. However, one thing never changes—the wonder that is Arches National Park.

[1] **resemble:** to look like

Name _____ Date _____

Be a Park Volunteer

Places across the United States are indebted to people who volunteer, or offer to do work without pay. The National Park Service has a program for people who want to help at a park. It is the VIP Program, which stands for Volunteers-in-Parks Program.

Volunteers from around the world come to work in U.S. parks. These people all want to protect and care for nature as well as the history of our country. Through their volunteer work, they meet new people and explore new places.

At Arches National Park, volunteers help in many ways. Trails need to be cared for to make them safe for hikers. Many park visitors want tour guides to hit the high points of interest at the park. Volunteers may scribble directions to certain arches for visitors. Other times, they may remind park visitors not to walk on the fragile[1] "living soil." Visiting Arches National Park can be like visiting another country with special rules.

Volunteer guides also give visitors important facts about the hidden dangers of the desert. The biggest dangers are the heat and the lack of available water. Volunteers are trained to help people who show signs of heat stress, helping them deal with it before it becomes worse. Volunteers also remind people that they can prevent heat problems by carrying lots of water on long trails.

In addition, some desert animals can be dangerous. Snakes, spiders, and scorpions are just a few of the animals that can ruin a park visit. Volunteers learn about these animals and help park visitors stay safe.

The National Park Service cannot hire enough people to give all of the services that park visitors need. Because of this, volunteers are critical to parks. If you want to volunteer, helping out in a park can be a great way to do it—just ask volunteer Raymond Santos. "My family visited Arches National Park on many different occasions," says Santos. "It is so rewarding to feel that I can give back to a place that has given so much to us."

[1] **fragile:** easily damaged or destroyed

Name _____ Date _____

Now answer Numbers 19 through 35 on your Answer Sheet. Base your answers on the articles "Arches National Park" and "Be a Park Volunteer."

19 Read the chart about the article "Arches National Park."

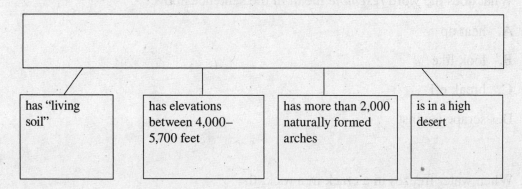

| has "living soil" | has elevations between 4,000–5,700 feet | has more than 2,000 naturally formed arches | is in a high desert |

Which idea best completes the chart?

A. average rainfall at Arches National Park

B. why arches form in Arches National Park

C. changing seasons at Arches National Park

D. interesting features of Arches National Park

20 Read this sentence from the article "Arches National Park."

> **Arches National Park in Utah is one of America's most interesting parks.**

Which word has the same sound as the underlined part of the word *parks*?

F. chart

G. dear

H. entire

I. stare

21 Read this sentence from the article "Arches National Park."

Thin sandstone walls resemble the fins on a fish's back.

What does the word *resemble* mean in the sentence above?

A. heat up

B. look like

C. break off

D. scrape against

22 When water freezes in a crack in a rock, the

F. rock breaks apart.

G. rock forms a thin wall.

H. water helps plants grow.

I. water runs to the ground.

23 Read this sentence from the article "Arches National Park."

Animals and vegetation must struggle to survive there.

What does the word *vegetation* mean in the sentence above?

A. plant life

B. living soil

C. black crust

D. tiny organisms

24 How does "living soil" benefit plants in Arches National Park?

F. It does not freeze.

G. It helps plants take root.

H. It does not damage easily.

I. It breaks up organisms in the soil.

25 Read this sentence from the article "Arches National Park."

> The "living soil" is a knobby, black crust made of living organisms that spreads across the ground and holds loose soil together, preventing wind and water erosion.

In the sentence above, the word *erosion* means the process by which

A. plants collect and use water.

B. soil loses important nutrients.

C. the earth's plant life reproduces.

D. the earth's surface is worn away.

26 Read this sentence from the article "Arches National Park."

> Even though the park today looks much like it has for thousands of years, appearances can be deceiving.

What does the author mean by the phrase *appearances can be deceiving* in the sentence above?

F. Change cannot be avoided.

G. Time can be a difficult thing to measure.

H. Things may look different than they actually are.

I. Things often have more in common than it seems at first.

27 Read this sentence from the article "Be a Park Volunteer."

> Places across the United States are indebted to people who volunteer, or offer to do work without pay.

How would the effect of this sentence be different if the author had used the words *helped by* instead of *indebted to*?

A. The volunteers would seem less available.

B. The volunteers would seem more well-off.

C. The volunteers would seem less important.

D. The volunteers would seem more demanding.

28 Read this sentence from the article "Be a Park Volunteer."

Volunteers may scribble directions to certain arches for visitors.

What words does the word *scribble* mean in the sentence above?

F. draw a pretty picture

G. mark points on a map

H. write down in a hurry

I. color outside the lines

29 Read this sentence from the article "Be a Park Volunteer."

Volunteer guides also give visitors important facts about the hidden dangers of the desert.

Which word has the same sound as the underlined part of the word *imp<u>or</u>tant*?

A. fur

B. hour

C. pear

D. roar

30 In "Be a Park Volunteer," how does the author support the idea that volunteers inform visitors about dangers in the desert?

F. The author explains some of the dangers and how volunteers are trained to help.

G. The author lists a number of ways that visitors can avoid running into desert dangers.

H. The author gives a detailed description of one specific danger visitors may encounter.

I. The author shares a story of how a volunteer helped some visitors escape from danger.

31 Read this sentence from the article "Be a Park Volunteer."

> **Volunteers also remind people that they can prevent heat problems by carrying lots of water on long trails.**

In the sentence above, the word *prevent* means

A. drink water.

B. cause to increase.

C. keep from happening.

D. allow air to enter into.

32 Why do volunteers learn about desert animals?

F. to keep visitors out of danger

G. to steer visitors to specific locations

H. to teach visitors about the living soil

I. to show visitors where to find wildlife

33 Read this sentence from the article

> **In addition, some desert animals can be dangerous.**

Which word has the same sound as the underlined part of the word *dangerous*?

A. bacteria

B. cheerful

C. coloring

D. furious

Name _____ Date _____

34 Read this sentence from the article "Be a Park Volunteer."

Because of this, volunteers are critical to parks.

What does the word *critical* mean in the sentence above?

F. unpaid

G. friendly

H. important

I. knowledgeable

35 The author includes the quotation at the end of "Be a Park Volunteer" to help readers understand

A. how volunteers become trained to help visitors.

B. what volunteers can gain from their experience.

C. that the National Park Service is hiring volunteers.

D. that national parks would have to close without volunteers.

Revising and Editing

Read the introduction and the article "All About Seahorses" before answering Numbers 1 through 7.

Paula wrote this article about seahorses. Read her article and think about the changes she should make.

All About Seahorses

(1) A seahorse is named for the shape of its head, which looked like that of a horse. (2) However, a seahorse is a kind of fish. (3) It has a straight body under its head. (4) At the top of its head, there is a part that looks like a crown. (5) A seahorse's crown is unique, similar to a human fingerprint. (6) Each seahorse has a different one.

(7) Not only is a seahorse like other fish, in that it breathes through gills, swims with fins, and is able to float. (8) It is also very different from other fish. (9) Most fish are covered with scales, but a seahorse has armer made from hard plates. (10) A seahorse uses its fins to balance, brake, move forward.

(11) A seahorse eats to survive small animals. (12) Most seahorses hunt for food during the day. (13) They sit still and wait for their prey. (14) They use their tails to hold onto plants. (15) These seahorses are hard to see because they blend in with the plants. (16) A seahorse does not have any teeth.

(17) Amanda Vincent is a marine scientist who studies seahorses.

(18) "Well" she says, when asked how many seahorses there are in the world, "no one actually knows." (19) They are also popular. (20) Because of this, people are working hard to make sure this special fish has a future.

Now answer Numbers 1 through 7 on your Answer Sheet. Base your answers on the changes Paula should make.

1 What change should be made in sentence 1?

   A. change *is* to **are**

   B. change *its* to **it's**

   C. delete the comma after *head*

   D. change *looked* to **looks**

2 What is the best way to revise sentences 7 and 8?

   F. Not only is a sea horse like other fish. In that it breathes through gills, swims with fins, and is able to float. It is also very different from other fish.

   G. Not only is a sea horse like other fish, in that it breathes through gills, swims with fins, and is able to float, or it is also very different from other fish.

   H. Not only is a sea horse like other fish, in that it breathes through gills, swims with fins, and is able to float, and it is also very different from other fish.

   I. Not only is a sea horse like other fish, in that it breathes through gills, swims with fins, and is able to float, but it is also very different from other fish.

3 What change should be made in sentence 9?

    A. change *covered* to **covering**

    B. change *but* to **and**

    C. change *armer* to **armor**

    D. change *hard* to **hardest**

4 What is the best way to revise sentence 10?

    F. A seahorse uses its fins to balance, brake, and move forward.

    G. A seahorse uses its fins to balance and brake, to move forward.

    H. A seahorse uses its fins to balance and brake and to move forward.

    I. A seahorse uses its fins to balance and brake and uses its fins to move forward.

5 What change should be made in sentence 11?

    A. insert a comma after *seahorse*

    B. change *eats* to **ate**

    C. change *to survive small animals* to **small animals to survive**

    D. change the period to a question mark

6 What is the best way to expand sentence 16?

    F. A seahorse does not have any teeth, which are found in the jaws.

    G. A seahorse does not have any teeth, so it must swallow food whole.

    H. A seahorse does not have any teeth, and it is found in tropical waters.

    I. A seahorse does not have any teeth, but some other fish don't have teeth either.

7 What is the best way to revise sentence 18?

A. "Well" she says, when asked how many seahorses there are in the world "no one actually knows."

B. "Well she says, when asked how many seahorses there are in the world, no one actually knows."

C. "Well," she says, "when asked how many seahorses there are in the world, no one actually knows."

D. "Well," she says, when asked how many seahorses there are in the world, "no one actually knows."

Read the introduction and the letter "A Computer Program" before answering Numbers 8 through 14.

Felicity has written a letter to her grandparents. Read her letter and think about the changes she should make.

A Computer Program

Dear Grandma and Grandpa,

(1) I cannot believe that the school year is almost over! (2) This has been one of my favorite years yet. (3) I have been astonished by how quickly the months have passed. (4) It's exactly like Mom says, "Wow time sure flies when you are having fun!"

(5) This summer, my school is offering an advanced program for a handful of fifth-grade students. (6) I am thrilled, I have been invited to participate in this program. (7) My teacher will be showing a variety of computer skills. (8) Mom and Dad told me that they are excited about me taking advantage of this really really really good opportunity.

(9) The program is six weeks long and will be held at the local community college. (10) We will attend classes Monday through Friday for four hours each day. (11) During the classes, I expect to learn many new things. (12) I will listen carefully. (13) I will take notes. (14) I will ask questions when I want to learn more about something.

(15) On the final day of class, our family members is allowed to accompany us. (16) It will be perfect timing because that is just when you will happen to be visiting us. (17) I cannot wait to teach you some of the things I have learned. (18) I am excited to show you how to write letters using e-mail,

Name _____ Date _____

which is an abbreviation for electronic mail. (19) You learn how to use e-mail,

and we can write each other much more frequently.

Love,

Felicity

_____

Now answer Numbers 8 through 14 on your Answer Sheet. Base your answers on the changes Felicity should make.

8 What change should be made in sentence 4?

F. change *It's* to **Its**

G. change *Mom* to **mom**

H. change the comma to a period

I. insert a comma after *Wow*

9 What is the best way to revise sentence 6?

A. I am thrilled until I have been invited to participate in this program.

B. While I am thrilled, I have been invited to participate in this program.

C. I am thrilled because I have been invited to participate in this program.

D. As a result, I am thrilled, I have been invited to participate in this program.

10 What change should be made in sentence 7?

F. change *My* to **Me**

G. change *will* to **was**

H. insert **us** after *showing*

I. insert a comma after *computer*

11 What change should be made in sentence 8?

    A. change *told* to **tells**

    B. change *they* to **them**

    C. change *really really really good* to **wonderful**

    D. change the period to a question mark

12 What is the best way to revise sentences 12–14?

    F. I will listen carefully, take notes, and ask questions when I want to learn more about something.

    G. I will listen carefully and taking notes and ask questions when I want to learn more about something.

    H. Listening carefully and taking notes, then I will ask questions when I want to learn more about something.

    I. I will listen carefully and take notes then I will ask questions when I want to learn more about something.

13 What change should be made in sentence 15?

    A. change *final* to **finally**

    B. change *is* to **are**

    C. insert *with* after *accompany*

    D. change *us* to **we**

14 What is the best way to revise sentence 19?

    F. So you learn how to use e-mail to write to each other much more frequently

    G. You learn how to use e-mail, we can write to each other much more frequently.

    H. When you learn how to use e-mail, we can write to each other much more frequently.

    I. We can write to each other much more frequently, so once you learn how to use e-mail.

Read the introduction and the passage "Paul Revere" before answering Numbers 15 through 20.

John wrote this passage about Paul Revere. Read his passage and think about the changes he should make.

Paul Revere

(1) I look at the calender hanging on the wall. (2) I see that today is April 16, 1775. (3) My friends John Hancock and Samuel Adams are now fugitives, in hiding. (4) These patriots have protested against British taxes. (5) They frequently spoke out against British rule. (6) Their actions and words greatly angered the king and the British Parliament.

(7) I know that the British troops will be searching for Hancock. (8) They will be searching for Adams. (9) I arranged for a fellow patriot to signal me so I will know when the British troops leave Boston.

(10) I said, "If the British leave by land, hang one lantern in the tower of the Old North Church all right?" (11) I also told him if they leave by sea—across the Charles River—he should hang two lanterns.

(12) On April 18, I saw two lanterns in the church tower.

(13) I knew this meant that the British troops were heading toward other Massachusetts towns, I quickly got on my horse. (14) Then I rode through the villages and across the land yelling, "The Regulars are coming out!" (15) I arrived in Lexington, I warned Adams and Hancock. (16) I was thankful that they were able to escape to the countryside before the British troops arrived.

(17) Now I'm waiting to meet up with William Dawes. (18) I expect him to arrive at midnight, when he and I will journey to Concord. (19) We will protect the important supplies that have been hidden there.

Name _____ Date _____

Now answer Numbers 15 through 20 on your Answer Sheet. Base your answers on the changes John should make.

15 What change should be made in sentence 1?

    A. change *calender* to **calendar**

    B. change *hanging* to **hanged**

    C. change *on* to **to**

    D. change *wall* to **Wall**

16 What is the best way to revise sentences 4 and 5?

    F. These patriots have protested against British taxes, frequently spoke out against British rule.

    G. These patriots have protested against British taxes, and these patriots frequently spoke out against British rule.

    H. Not only have these patriots protested against British taxes, but they also frequently spoke out against British rule.

    I. In addition to these patriots protesting against British taxes, these patriots frequently speaking out against British rule.

17 What is the best way to revise sentences 7 and 8?

    A. I know that the British troops will be searching for Hancock and Adams.

    B. I know that the British troops will be searching: for Hancock and for Adams.

    C. I know that the British troops, for Hancock and for Adams, will be searching.

    D. I know that the British troops will be searching for Hancock, also searching for Adams.

18 What change should be made in sentence 10?

    F. change *said* to **says**

    G. change *one* to **won**

    H. insert a comma after *Church*

    I. change the question mark to a period

19 What change should be made in sentence 13?

    A. change *that* to **which**

    B. insert **so** after *towns,*

    C. change *got* to **get**

    D. insert a comma after *horse*

20 What is the best way to revise sentence 15?

    F. I arrived in Lexington, if I warned Adams and Hancock.

    G. I arrived in Lexington, and I warned Adams and Hancock.

    H. I arrived in Lexington, after I warned Adams and Hancock.

    I. I arrived in Lexington, although I warned Adams and Hancock.

STOP

Name _____ Date _____

Writing to Inform

Read the prompt and plan your response.

Most people have an object that has a special meaning for them.

Think about an object that has a special meaning for you.

Now write an essay explaining what this object is and why it has a special meaning for you.

Planning Page

Use this space to make your notes before you begin writing. The writing on this page will NOT be scored.

_____

_____

_____

_____

_____

_____

_____

_____

_____

_____

_____

_____

Name _____ Date _____

Begin writing your response here. The writing on this page and the next page WILL be scored.

_____

_____

_____

_____

_____

_____

_____

_____

_____

_____

_____

_____

_____

_____

_____

_____

_____

_____

_____

_____

Name _____ Date _____

Name _____ Date _____

Reading Complex Text

Read the article "It's Called Poetry Slam." As you read, stop and answer each question. Use evidence from the article to support your answers.

It's Called Poetry Slam

The arena is the stage. The wrestlers are poets. The match is words—not just any words, though: spoken poetry. Grab your popcorn and take your seats because the words are about to fly. You are about to see a unique art form; it's called poetry slam.

Poetry Slam? What's *That*?

Poetry slam is competitive performance poetry. For the poets who participate, "slammin'" is about composing a poem and then serving it up to the audience. It's as much about the performance—the act of breathing life into the poem—as it is about the written words. In a poetry slam, the live performance is all-important. A poem that could vie for a Nobel Prize can wither and die in front of a live audience. On the other hand, a poet who delivers a simple, short, and funny poem with lots of energy can knock off an audience's socks.

---

❶ In addition to how well a poem is written, what helps a poet win in a poetry slam?

_____

_____

_____

The Roots of Poetry Slam

Poetry slam is really just a new spin on a long-lived tradition. It would be hard to pinpoint a culture on the planet that does *not* have oral tradition and performance poetry at its roots. From West Africa to the early Americas to ancient Greece, poetry helped ancient peoples memorize and pass down their oral history. The competition aspect is not a modern idea either. Poetry competitions were held at festivals in ancient Greece. During the fifteenth century, Japanese poet Bashō played referee at haiku contests.

Poetry slam, as it is commonly known today, originated at a Chicago jazz club in the mid-1980s. Bored with the usual poetry readings, which drew few audience members, a group of poets felt the need to spice things up. They decided that adding a performance aspect might just do the trick. Later, they added another aspect: competition. Poetry slam was born! In 1990, San Francisco hosted the first-ever National Poetry Slam competition. Every year, hosting honors are passed like a torch from city to city. Poetry slams are popular at the local level, too. With a few key ingredients and a little bit of planning, anyone can organize a poetry slam in their community.

> **2** How does the author support the idea that poetry competitions have a long history? Give one example from the text.
>
> _____
>
> _____
>
> _____

How It Works

A poetry slam is run like a contest, with a winner crowned at the end of the event. But it is important to keep in mind that the spirit of a slam is about performance, entertainment and, yes, the poetry.

The general rules. Like any contest, a poetry slam operates by an agreed-upon set of rules. Some of these rules may vary from slam to slam, but generally speaking, here they are, short and sweet:

1. Each poet must read his or her original work. If you aspire to be a "slammer," start writing!

2. Each poem must be read in three minutes or less. If you're a fan of epic poems, you'll have to take your long-winded art somewhere else.

3. No props or costumes may be used. The only things poets get to bring onstage are their words.

The basics of judging. The poets are not the only ones who participate in a poetry slam. Some listeners are selected as judges. They get to rate the poems and declare a verdict—the winner. It is the poet's obligation to entertain and inspire the audience; it is the judges' job to evaluate the quality of the poem and its delivery. The basics of judging for poetry slams are as follows:

✓ Typically, "slam" judges are selected at random from the audience. The judges aren't trained literary critics; they're just regular people, out to enjoy a bit of word-sport. Just like their tastes for food and movies, their tastes for poetry probably differ.

✓ After each performance, judges each toss out a score, ranging from 0–10. Judges are allowed, even encouraged, to use decimal points to lessen the chance of a tie.

✓ Among five judges, the highest and lowest scores are thrown out. The middle three scores are added up. A really dazzling, roof-raising performance could earn a top score of 30.

✓ Judges rate poets on their actual poetry and on their performance. *How* those words tumble out of the poet's mouth is as important as the words themselves.

Name _____ Date _____

As a member of the audience, don't expect to sit in hushed silence throughout the poetry slam. The audience at a poetry slam is encouraged to get involved, too—to clap, cheer, and express their approval or, as the case may be, disapproval.

3 Explain what happens at a poetry slam.

_____

_____

_____

Poetry slam is a great way to liven up your school or a local café. The ingredients can be found most anywhere. Round up some budding poets, a group of enthusiastic listeners, and converge on a scene of your choice. Then, let the slamming begin.

4 What are two main ideas in this passage? Tell one key detail the author uses to support each main idea.

_____

_____

_____

_____

_____

Reading and Analyzing Text

Read the passage "On the Job" before answering Numbers 1 through 6.

On the Job

When my sister Penny left home for the university this past year, I inherited quite a few of her things. The most appreciated was her bedroom, because now I no longer occupy a room with a little brother in it. Another thing I inherited was her baseball glove, with its comfortable leather that's broken in just the way I like it, and I'm especially loving the boxed set of medieval dragon books that wouldn't quite fit in her suitcase.

This story is not about any of that, however; it's about something else that Penny handed down to me: her babysitting job at the Andersons. I'll have to admit, I was more than a little excited about it. My friend Paolo began watching his neighbor's children after school every Wednesday about the middle of the winter, and he already has an impressive savings account. And all from babysitting—I mean, how difficult could babysitting possibly be?

Penny had been sitting for the Andersons ever since she was in the seventh grade, when there was just a pair of newborn twins, Sophie and Anne. Now, the girls are six, and they have a two-year-old brother named Max. The kids are adorable—I know because Penny dragged me over there sometimes to help her out. I also took a babysitting workshop at the local community center last semester. Therefore, I arrived for my first assignment confident and feeling a bit like a veteran.

It was a Friday afternoon. Mr. Anderson was still at his business, and Mrs. Anderson was working, too, in her home office on the second floor. She greeted me at the door with Max propped on her hip. "Hello, Jeff!" she said, a bit tiredly. "The girls are both so excited to see you."

Where are they? I wondered, but as soon as I stepped inside the doorway, I got my answer as a twin flew at me from each side, grabbing my legs and wrestling me all the way to the carpet. When I finally regained my feet, the girls were still plastered to my legs.

"No physical stuff inside, girls," scolded Mrs. Anderson. "You know that." She rattled off a few more rules before handing Max to me and going upstairs to continue with her work.

No more than an inch from my face, Max was staring at me as though he had never seen a middle-school boy in his entire life; however, when he was ready to speak, he spoke. "Doose bock!"

It must have taken me a full minute to translate, but eventually we were on our way to the refrigerator for a juice box. When we got there, I was confronted with a room that looked nothing like the immaculate kitchen I had seen earlier, when Mrs. Anderson gave me the tour. Every cabinet door was open—underneath the sink, beside the automatic dishwasher, and over the counters. Mixing bowls were scattered all across the floor.

Name _____ Date _____

"We're cooking!" Sophie announced proudly, holding up an enormous mixing bowl while Anne poured in a purplish powder.

"Uh . . . I think we'll have to see about that." I figured out what was going on—the girls were testing my limits. I had intended not to set any limits—I wanted these kids to like me. I wanted to be "the coolest babysitter." However, cooking, I reasoned, was obviously unsafe.

"You know you're not allowed to cook," I told them as I deposited Max in his kiddie seat at the table.

"Well, it's not *cooking*, really," said Anne. "It's only instant pudding." Clumsily, she dumped almost a cup of milk mostly into the bowl. "You stir it, Sophie, and I'll go get the mixer."

"Whoa, whoa, WHOA! No way are you using an electric appliance."

"It's not even electric," said Anne, with a somewhat superior attitude, and with that, she handed an old-fashioned eggbeater to Sophie, who plunged it deep into the mixing bowl and cranked the handle ferociously.

Suddenly, there was an alarming crash. I turned to discover Max sitting on the floor banging two lids into one another.

"Max—you put those down right now!" Anne stomped over to take the lids away, which set Max screaming. Sophie, still cranking the eggbeater ferociously, turned toward the commotion. This movement caused the eggbeater to elevate above the lip of the bowl, with Sophie still cranking the handle, still cranking it ferociously.

"Watch it!" I shouted, but it was too late: clumps of chocolate pudding flew everywhere and stuck where they landed. Amid the mess, I suddenly imagined Penny being with me. *You'd better get complete control of this situation immediately,* she would say. That advice was more than enough for me. "All right, listen everybody," I commanded. "We're going to start cleaning up this mess, this instant!"

"You're not any fun at all," Anne pouted, hiding a grin.

"Penny always let us make our own pudding," Sophie complained, also with an undercover grin.

"Not without asking permission first." I had them there.

"Sorry," said the girls, and they began to put away the pots.

I switched on the countertop radio. "Let's do our work to music." I realized then that a babysitting course couldn't teach me everything I needed to know; the remainder, I was going to have to learn on the job. As the twins and I cleaned and danced, Max toddled over and hugged my leg. At that moment, I felt like Penny's old job was officially mine.

Now answer Numbers 1 through 6 on your Answer Sheet. Base your answers on the passage "On the Job."

 Read this dictionary entry.

> **admit** (ad-MIHT) *verb*
>
> 1. to allow to enter
> 2. to acknowledge or confess as true
> 3. to have or leave room for
> 4. to allow participation in

Read this sentence from the passage.

I'll have to admit, I was more than a little excited about it.

Which meaning best fits the way the word *admit* is used in the sentence above?

A. meaning 1

B. meaning 2

C. meaning 3

D. meaning 4

2 Which detail from the passage best explains why Jeff feels excited about taking over his sister's babysitting job?

   F. Jeff sometimes went with Penny to the Andersons.

   G. Jeff's friend Paolo saved lots of money from his babysitting job.

   H. Penny had been sitting for the Andersons since the seventh grade.

   I. The Andersons have six-year-old twin girls and a two-year-old boy.

3 Read this sentence from the passage.

> **Therefore, I arrived for my first assignment confident and feeling a bit like a veteran.**

What does this statement mean?

   A. Jeff thinks children are like animals.

   B. The Andersons' house is like a war zone.

   C. Jeff feels that he's an experienced babysitter.

   D. The Andersons like to give the babysitter homework.

4 Why do Anne and Sophie apologize to Jeff towards the end of the passage?

   F. They realize they hurt his feelings.

   G. They feel badly about lying to Jeff.

   H. They scolded Max and made him cry.

   I. They know they did not ask permission to cook.

5 How do the first three paragraphs help the author set up the main action of the passage?

   A. The narrator shares some of the babysitting advice that Penny left him.

   B. The narrator explains how he landed the babysitting job at the Andersons.

   C. The narrator tells about an event that made him decide to start babysitting.

   D. The narrator describes the Anderson family and the children's personalities.

6 As the girls make a mess and Max bangs the pot lids, Jeff takes control because he

    F. imagines what Penny would tell him to do.

    G. is afraid that Mrs. Anderson will hear the noise.

    H. wants the children to think that he is a fun babysitter.

    I. sees clumps of chocolate pudding flying and sticking everywhere.

Read the article "The Wettest Place on Earth" before answering Numbers 7 through 13.

The
WETTEST
PLACE
on Earth
by Sherrill Kushner

One of the places in the world with the most rain is in India. In some years, the town of Cherrapunji (Chair-ah-POON-jee) is the rainiest. In other years, its neighbor, the town of Mawsynram (maw-sin-RAHM), gets the most rain.

It once rained in Cherrapunji every day for almost two years. In 1861, it got the most rain in a month and the most in a year (1,041 inches), setting world records. Today, the towns receive an average of 366 inches of rain a year. That's nearly eight times as much as the average rainfall in New York City (47 inches) and 24 times as much as Los Angeles (15 inches).

Yet the people living in these towns in India don't have enough water to drink, to bathe, and to cook their meals. Why does it rain so much there, and why is water so scarce?

The extreme rainfall occurs because the towns are high above ground, near an ocean, and in the path of a special wind system called a monsoon. Air is drawn in from the Indian Ocean and blows over the plains below the two towns that are located almost one mile above sea level. As the air rises, it cools, picks up moisture, and forms rain clouds. In spring and summer, the monsoon blows up from the valley below and releases its rain in Cherrapunji and Mawsynram. The heaviest downpours come with stinging force between April and September.

So why is there a shortage of water? People have harmed the environment over time by cutting down trees, mining for coal and limestone, and growing crops in ways that have caused the topsoil to wash away. The land has become dry and stony. Without forests or topsoil, the rain doesn't sink into the ground to fill underground wells. Also, there is a six-month dry season from October to the following April, when the monsoon reverses direction away from these towns. During that time, trees and vegetation have difficulty growing.

It is also hard to store the rain. The downpour is so heavy that the riverbanks and levees can't hold all the water. The levees break and the rainwater races downhill over high cliffs. Water floods the neighboring country of Bangladesh below.

80

The towns of Cherrapunji and Mawsynram are very poor and far from other communities. They cannot afford to repair rusty, cracked storage tanks and leaky pipes that carried water from other places. So the people of Cherrapunji put out buckets to catch the water during the rainy season. In the dry winter, women and children carry empty oilcans on their backs and trek miles uphill to bring water from the springs above the town. This takes several hours and the cans are heavy. Sometimes the townspeople can buy water from containers on trucks that are driven up from the plains below.

Too much rain means flooding — a common occurence in Cherrapunji.

"Water, water everywhere, nor any drop to drink," wrote poet Samuel Taylor Coleridge in a famous poem about being on the ocean. This could also describe the wettest place on Earth.

Now answer Numbers 7 through 13 on your Answer Sheet. Base your answers on the article "The Wettest Place on Earth."

7 During the months from October to the next April in Cherrapunji and Mawsynram

    A. very little rain falls.

    B. crops and trees grow well.

    C. the people store extra water.

    D. miners dig for coal and limestone.

8 Weather patterns affect life in Cherrapunji and Mawsynram by making these towns

    F. very green.

    G. important for trade.

    H. hard places to survive.

    I. good areas for mining.

9 According to the article, which of the following is one of the wettest places in the world?

   A. India

   B. Bangladesh

   C. Los Angeles

   D. New York City

10 Read this sentence from the article.

> Sometimes the townspeople can buy water from containers on trucks that are driven up from the plains below.

The word *containers* comes from the Latin root *tain* meaning to

   F. build.

   G. come.

   H. hold.

   I. turn.

11 The main cause of the high rainfall in Cherrapunji and Mawsynram is that

   A. the towns are close to one another.

   B. the people have cut down most of the trees.

   C. the monsoon blows directly across the towns.

   D. the water in the ocean is evaporating at a high rate.

12 The people of Cherrapunji and Mawsynram cannot repair storage tanks and pipes because they

   F. have too little time.

   G. have too little money.

   H. get too much rainfall.

   I. live too far from other towns.

Name _____ Date _____

13 Read this sentence from the article.

> **"Water, water everywhere, nor any drop to drink," wrote poet Samuel Taylor Coleridge in a famous poem about being on the ocean.**

In what way does this saying also describe the towns of Cherrapunji and Mawsynram?

A. The towns are very close to the Indian Ocean, but in many months of the year, it rarely rains.

B. The towns are able to collect lots of water when it rains, but people cannot drink the water.

C. The towns receive more rain than any place in the world, but there is a water shortage in the towns.

D. The towns collect lots of water from springs above the towns, but water is not available for people to buy.

Read the articles "Maria Mitchell, Astronomer and Teacher" and "An Interview with Maria Mitchell" before answering Numbers 14 through 19.

Maria Mitchell, Astronomer and Teacher

"The eye that directs the needle," astronomer Maria Mitchell observed, "will equally well bisect a star. . . ." The eye she referred to was that of women, almost all of whom knew how to sew back when Maria Mitchell was born in 1818. However, Maria believed that women could also do much more than oversee a household. The third of ten children in a Quaker family in Massachusetts, Maria grew up in a home where learning was part of living. Most people of that era thought girls didn't need academics. Yet Maria's parents taught all of their children to learn just for the sheer love of knowledge.

Her father recognized Maria's talent for mathematics and science. He taught her celestial navigation to set ships' clocks and to observe the stars. Maria was just twelve when she helped her father record an eclipse. As a teen, she spent countless nights watching the sky from the roof of their home. These interests were unusual for young women of her day. Few studied the sciences or mathematics. Fewer still became physicians or researchers. But change was happening ever so slowly. During her life, Maria worked as a scientist and as a teacher to lead that change.

On October 1, 1847, Maria really made her mark in astronomy. As she watched the sky through her father's telescope, a comet sped into her field of view. She knew at once how important her sighting was. She was the first person to record a comet sighting. She had done something truly remarkable. She had discovered a comet using only a telescope.

Fame followed Maria's discovery, and she received a gold medal for her work. She also became the first female member of the American Academy of Arts and Sciences. She met many other scientists and talked about her work with them. Still, she knew that men of science did not think of her as a real scientist. They failed to take her work seriously. History showed so few examples of women in science.

Maria understood that a woman scientist was an alien idea to people. She wanted to change this perception and show them she was not unique. She wanted people to know that other women could also become scientists. At seventeen, Maria had set up a small school to teach girls math and science. Now, older and better known, she began teaching at Vassar, the first women's college in the United States.

She was a challenging and entertaining teacher. She held "dome parties" in the astronomy building. Any student could come to these gatherings and look through the telescope, play games, and tell amusing stories. Over the years, many students were touched by her love of science, as well as her friendship.

Name _____ Date _____

Teaching at the college was sometimes difficult, partly because so little money was available to buy science equipment. Maria received a telescope only after women across the nation raised and donated money to buy it. And she earned less than the young male teachers who had not yet done notable research. The college finally increased her salary when she brought the unfairness to their attention.

Over the years, Maria actually saw changes in how the nation perceived[1] women in the sciences. By the time of her death, in 1889, higher numbers of women were studying more branches of science than ever before. It would have pleased her to know that women were taking action and acquiring knowledge for themselves.

[1] **perceived:** thought of, understood

Vassar Student Newsletter

September 22, 1871

An Interview with Maria Mitchell, Professor of Astronomy at Vassar College

Interviewer: Professor Mitchell, you were the first female member of the prestigious American Association for the Advancement of Science. How did you become a member?

Maria Mitchell: Well, it started with what now seems like kind of a fluke event. You see, I was the first person to see a comet through a telescope. I remember it was 1847, and I was working as the librarian in Nantucket, Massachusetts, where my family is from. I took that job because I knew I would have great access to literature and scientific books. My father was an astronomer and a teacher. He had taught me astronomy during my childhood, and it remained one of my passions as an adult.

Anyway, my father owned a telescope, and after my days working at the library, I would come home and spend evenings peering though the telescope to observe the stars and sky. For several evenings before I saw the comet, I had been focused on a pair of stars that had no relationship to the comet. I really wasn't even looking for a comet. But then, one evening, I noticed strange light near the North Star. Of course, I knew the skies very well, because my father had instructed me and it was one of my passions. I knew right away that something interesting was happening. My father and I discussed it, and we soon realized it was an undiscovered comet.

Interviewer: So you were made a member of the American Association for the Advancement of Science after that?

Maria Mitchell: Yes. After we determined that it was an undiscovered comet, we notified several astronomers. As it turns out, the King of Denmark had offered a gold medal to the person who first discovered a comet that was only visible through a telescope. My sighting was the first, and they named the comet "Miss Mitchell's Comet." My discovery was featured in a journal, and word of my work spread. Eventually, it caught the attention of the people at the American Association for the Advancement of Science. After some protest, I was elected a member.

Interviewer: What kind of protest?

Maria Mitchell: Well, as you know, there were not a lot of women researchers and scientists then. A number of people thought that there shouldn't be women researchers or scientists. But although some may have been unhappy about it, I was elected all the same, based on the quality of my work and discoveries.

You know, the opening of Vassar College wasn't that different. Vassar was the first endowed college for women, and there was strong resistance to opening it. Some critics of the college said that it would completely ruin the country. Vassar was opened in 1861. In the last ten years, it's become a very good school, and I can't imagine anyone believing it's ruined the country or anything silly like that. Just as with my election to the association, it's not about whether you are male or female. It's about the work that you do, and your contributions to your field.

Now answer Numbers 14 through 19 on your Answer Sheet. Base your answers on the articles "Maria Mitchell, Astronomer and Teacher" and "An Interview with Maria Mitchell."

14 Read this sentence from the article "Maria Mitchell, Astronomer and Teacher."

> **"The eye that directs the needle," astronomer Maria Mitchell observed, "will equally well bisect a star . . ."**

Why does the author use the quotation in the first sentence of the article?

F. to introduce the idea that women had never before studied astronomy and other sciences

G. to introduce the idea that Maria Mitchell was nothing like traditional women of her time

H. to introduce the idea that women, like Maria Mitchell, were capable of studying astronomy

I. to introduce the idea that Maria Mitchell and other women of her time learned many different household tasks

15 Read this sentence from the article "Maria Mitchell, Astronomer and Teacher."

> **He taught her celestial navigation to set ship's clocks and to observe the stars.**

What does the word *celestial* mean in the sentence above?

A. relating to time

B. relating to history

C. relating to research and study

D. relating to the sky or outer space

16 Read this sentence from the newsletter interview with Maria Mitchell.

> **Some critics of the college said that it would completely ruin the country.**

What does the word *critics* mean in the sentence above?

F. people who find fault

G. people who make decisions

H. people who are involved in politics

I. people who don't believe in science

17 Which of the following best tells how the accounts of Mitchell spotting the comet in the article and in the newsletter interview differ?

A. In the article, the account discusses why Mitchell's sighting was important, while the newsletter interview does not.

B. In the article, the account is told by a firsthand observer. In the newsletter interview, the account is reported by the interviewer.

C. In the article, the account is told secondhand by the author. In the newsletter, the account is told in first-person, as if by Mitchell herself.

D. In the article, the account includes lots of sensory detail, while the account in the newsletter interview is told in a more factual way.

18 Unlike the newsletter interview with Maria Mitchell, which uses a question and answer format, the article "Maria Mitchell, Astronomer and Teacher" uses

F. chronological order.

G. a cause-and-effect structure.

H. a problem-solution structure.

I. a comparison-contrast structure.

19 According to the information in both the article and the newsletter interview, why did Maria Mitchell face resistance from some other scientists?

   A. They did not believe she had actually sighted a comet.

   B. They did not believe that women could become real scientists.

   C. They did not believe she had enough education to be a scientist.

   D. They did not believe she should become a teacher of astronomy.

Read the passage "The Case of the Vanishing TVs" before answering Numbers 20 through 24.

The Case of the Vanishing TVs

by Kristin O'Donnell Tubb
art by Brian Lies

My green pal Sal and I have drummed up a ton of business thanks to the ad we placed in the phone book:

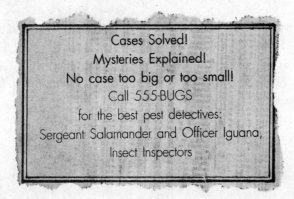

Cases Solved!
Mysteries Explained!
No case too big or too small!
Call 555-BUGS
for the best pest detectives:
Sergeant Salamander and Officer Iguana,
Insect Inspectors

Our latest case is a robbery at Acme Warehouse, where three television sets disappeared right off the shelves last night. Wayne, a husky-sounding wasp who manages the warehouse, called us with a few details at 7:00 A.M. He wanted us at their warehouse before the Acme employees started arriving at 8:00.

"Vanishing TVs!" Sal shouted, as he does every time we land a new case. "That means disappearing dramas! Stolen sitcoms! Missing mysteries! C'mon, Iggy!" And with that, he bounced outside and into our red convertible, gunning the engine.

I lumbered behind him, eventually pulling all six feet of myself into our cramped car. "We've gotta get a minivan," I mumbled.

"We've gotta get a move on!" Sal yelled, and we roared out of our parking space and sped toward Acme Warehouse.

Two minutes later, we screeched to a halt in front of Acme's large, windowless building. "You see, Iggy, warehouses simply house televisions temporarily, until the stores need more," Sal was explaining to me. "They're like really big attics, and they hold everything from bicycles to cans of soda pop."

"So they probably have lots of security, right?" I asked.

Name _____ Date _____

"Right," interrupted a musclebound wasp standing behind us. I would've been shaking in my shoes if I hadn't already known that our contact on this case was a wasp. "That's why we think it had to be one of our own employees, unfortunately. Employees know all the security codes and have keys to the building. I'm Wayne," he said, extending one of his four hands for a handshake. "Let's go inside and look around before the employees get here."

As we entered, I whistled as I looked at floor-to-ceiling shelves holding every item you can imagine. "It'd be easy to get lost in here!"

"Yeah. This building is over 20,000 square feet. We could fit ten large houses in here!" he said with a waspy grin.

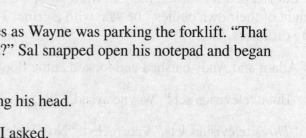

"So could the televisions simply have been misplaced?" Sal asked. It was a good question; trying to find three televisions in here would be like trying to find three Popsicle sticks in a haystack.

"No, probably not," Wayne explained. "The television sets are heavy and are on very high shelves, so it takes a forklift"—Wayne pointed to a vehicle that looked like a golf cart with arms—"to lift them. Watch."

We watched as Wayne steered the forklift, plucking a television set off a high shelf and lowering it to the ground.

"Look." I pointed to one of the shelves as Wayne was parking the forklift. "That shelf is damaged. Could a forklift do that?" Sal snapped open his notepad and began writing furiously.

"Yeah, maybe," Wayne said, scratching his head.

"So who has access to the forklifts?" I asked.

"That's just it. Only two of our employees—Adam and Andy, twin brothers—have keys to the forklifts, and both of them turned in their keys last night before they left. And the TVs were definitely in the right spot when all keys were accounted for at the end of the day."

"Did anyone leave work late?" I asked.

Wayne frowned. "I saw Adam and Andy in the parking lot around 5:30. Our shift ends at 5:00."

Name _____ Date _____

Sal scratched his head with his pencil. "Mind if we talk to those two?"

"Not at all," Wayne said, pointing at a couple of ants entering the warehouse across the huge room, lunchpails in hand. "Adam and Andy are two of our most loyal employees. They'll answer any questions you have."

"Ants! Well, Wayne, why didn't you just say so?" Sal laughed.

Wayne and I looked at each other, confused. "I believe my first question for them will be, 'Where are the television sets?' I don't think they've wandered very far."

"Well, yes, we *did* move three television sets," Adam stammered, looking a little scared. "But they're in the next aisle, see?" Andy pointed them out to us. The sets were on a shelf under a sign that said "microwaves."

"We know they don't belong there, but we put them there until we had the chance to talk to Wayne this morning," Andy added.

"They're so heavy, and the shelf they were on looked like it was going to topple." Adam pointed at the bent shelf. "It looked so unsafe."

Wayne still looked puzzled. "But how did you move them? You turned in your forklift keys last evening at 5:00!"

Sal stepped forward. "Ants can lift a *lot* of weight—fifty times the weight of their own bodies," he said with a grin. "They can carry it for long distances, too."

Adam and Andy blushed and looked at the floor.

"But a television set?" Wayne asked. "It's *so* heavy!"

"*Three* television sets," I corrected. "No problem for this pair. They can carry so much weight for their size that it would be like a human being carrying a compact car for five miles."

"Really?" Wayne asked, beaming with pride at his employees. They nodded.

Wayne turned to us. "Sorry for calling you in for nothing, inspectors. I guess that's what they call making a mountain out of an anthill!"

Now answer Numbers 20 through 24 on your Answer Sheet. Base your answers on the passage "The Case of the Vanishing TVs."

20 Read this sentence from the passage.

> **My green pal Sal and I have drummed up a ton of business thanks to the ad we placed in the phonebook . . .**

What does the phrase *drummed up* mean in the sentence above?

F. listened

G. played

H. produced

I. solved

21 Read this sentence from the passage.

> **"So could the televisions simply have been misplaced?" Sal asked.**

What is the meaning of the word *misplaced* as it is used in the sentence above?

A. not put in place

B. put in place first

C. put in place again

D. put in the wrong place

22 Why is the scene in which Wayne demonstrates how forklifts are used to lift television sets important to the passage?

F. It shows why Adam and Andy were hired to operate the forklifts for the warehouse.

G. It explains why only certain employees at the warehouse have access to the forklift keys.

H. It explains why Wayne is so concerned about the missing televisions and why he wants to find them.

I. It shows how heavy the televisions are and how impressive it is that Adam and Andy carried them.

Name _____ Date _____

23 What factual information about ants is necessary to this passage?

    A. Some ants are very muscular.

    B. Every ant has one twin sibling.

    C. All ants can lift much more than their body weight.

    D. Some ants work from around 9:00 A.M. to 5:00 P.M.

24 Unlike Sal, when Wayne finds out what the ants did, he is

    F. confused by how they moved the TVs.

    G. angry because they had moved the TVs.

    H. worried about them having carried such heavy items.

    I. sorry for them because they are embarrassed to be caught.

Read the passage "Hi, Neighbor" before answering Numbers 25 through 29.

Hi, Neighbor

The first I saw of Mrs. Kehoe was her feet when she walked around a tight circle of giant rose bushes where I was hiding. I was not hiding from Mrs. Kehoe; I was hiding from my parents. They had made me move away from my friends and my comfortable old neighborhood to this new street in a different part of town where I *knew* I would never find new friends. Frankly, hiding seemed pretty immature. Plus, hiding was more boring than I remembered.

"You there, I spy you hiding in my rose bushes," said a powerful voice from somewhere above the feet, which, by the way, were wearing sturdy black gardening clogs. "Come out now."

I crawled out sheepishly with scratches from the rose bush's thorns. Beyond that, I knew there were probably leaves throughout my hair and dirt on my knees and elbows.

"Hello, I'm Emily," I said, standing up and holding out my hand. "I just moved in next door."

"Into the old Foster place. That's good, very good," she said, shaking my hand firmly. "We need some children around here to liven things up. How old are you? About eleven?" I nodded my agreement. "You don't seem afraid to get dirty, Emily, which is an excellent quality. I'm Mrs. Kehoe, and these are my bushes. Here," she said, handing me a gardening tool I'd never seen before. It wasn't your basic rake or shovel or anything. It was a small tool that had a short, curved pair of blades at the end. When you worked the handles like a pair of scissors, the blades opened and closed like a snapping turtle's jaws. "Now, Emily," said Mrs. Kehoe, "we're going to prune these rose bushes. They need pruning in order to breathe correctly, and *you* need something useful to do until your parents decide to come looking for you."

What could I do but obey? She seemed so sure of everything, and it was oddly relaxing and refreshing to do something other than my usual chores.

As it turned out, Mrs. Kehoe knew a great deal about roses. It also turned out there was a lot to know. The bushes making up the circle I hid in were Buck roses, named after Griffith Buck, a man who'd spent most of his life teaching at a college in Iowa. His official subject had been engineering (a dry subject, Mrs. Kehoe noted), but, in all of his spare time, he grew and bred his roses. Over dozens of years, he had planted different roses in a field on his property, and those that survived the harsh Iowa winters were the ones he continued to breed. Roses were his passion, and he had been dedicated to breeding hardy and colorful versions. "I cannot stress enough the importance of passion and dedication, Emily," Mrs. Kehoe said. "That is the secret of satisfaction, which, my dear, you may find is more important than fame or greatness." By the end of Mr. Buck's very productive life, she continued, he had developed many different kinds of hardy, healthy, vivid roses. Any one of these roses, Mrs. Kehoe

95

assured me, would make a fine lifelong companion in the garden. We pruned a bush together, meaning she pointed, I cut. We were just about to start on a second bush when my mother ran breathlessly into Mrs. Kehoe's yard.

"Emily!" she said, "Are you bothering Mrs. Kehoe?"

"Not at all," Mrs. Kehoe said. "She's a good little pruner, and I hope," she said to me, "that you'll come back, because we have several more bushes to do."

I said that I would, and the truth is, I was looking forward to it.

As my mother dragged me by the hand towards my new yard, a yard that could really use a few Buck roses, I kept glancing back at Mrs. Kehoe in her large woven sunhat and her black clogs.

"Emily!" she yelled at me, waving a dark magenta rose that looked perfectly open and full, "the name of this specific Buck rose is 'Hi, Neighbor'!"

I laughed and waved my other hand.

Now answer Numbers 25 through 29 on your Answer Sheet. Base your answers on the passage "Hi, Neighbor."

25 Read this sentence from the passage.

> **Frankly, hiding seemed pretty immature.**

If *mature* means "adult-like" what does the word *immature* mean in the sentence above?

A. not adult-like

B. resembling an adult

C. in an adult-like way

D. becoming more adult-like

26 Read this sentence from the passage.

> **When you worked the handles like a pair of scissors, the blades opened and closed like a snapping turtle's jaws.**

The comparison of the tool's blades to a snapping turtle's jaws helps the reader understand that the tool is

   F. alive.

   G. green.

   H. small.

   I. strong.

27 Which of the following shows how Emily's thinking changes as she prunes roses with Mrs. Kehoe?

   A. She realizes she can make new friends.

   B. She learns that gardens make people happy.

   C. She decides that pruning is too difficult for her.

   D. She learns that obeying her parents is important.

28 According to Mrs. Kehoe, the result of Griffith Buck's hard work and dedication was that he developed

   F. a better method of pruning roses.

   G. a better tool with which to prune roses.

   H. many different kinds of strong, beautiful roses.

   I. a way to grow roses during harsh Iowa winters.

29 What is the main reason Emily is happy at the end of the passage?

   A. She has made a new friend.

   B. She likes her new neighborhood.

   C. She likes to play in the rose bushes.

   D. She has learned about Griffith Buck.

97

Read the article "Clichés" before answering Numbers 30 through 35.

Clichés

Raining cats and dogs

A cliché is a saying that is used so often it sounds stale and tired. The word itself comes from the print shop. In printing, a cliché is a wood or metal print block used to print the same word or picture again and again. Writers make their writing fresh and interesting by avoiding clichés. But avoiding them can be difficult because clichés are everywhere. And, everyone uses them! Consider a few of the clichés that come from just one word, *dog*.

Some dog clichés are used as advice. Being told to "let sleeping dogs lie" means you should leave a situation alone. Just as a dog may bark loudly if someone wakes him, sometimes a situation will worsen if a person continues to try to change it. To "dog someone's heels" means to follow someone closely, as a dog follows its owner.

Another popular cliché is about human behavior. "You can't teach an old dog new tricks" may not be true, however. Older people can indeed learn "new tricks." They take up painting, start new careers, or learn Chinese on a regular basis. Still, the cliché hangs on. Sometimes people are unwilling to change and use this cliché to refer to themselves.

Some dog clichés refer to historic fashions. Dressing up is called "putting on the dog." At one time men wore stiff, high collars, known then as dog collars. On the other hand, a person who is lazy or whose life is in disorder is sometimes said to have "gone to the dogs." Supposedly, a dog's life is mostly about sleeping and eating and playing, not about working.

Another dog cliché describes weather. People refer to the hottest days of summer as the "dog days." This cliché came from the ancient Romans. They noticed that the star Sirius shone brightly during the hot summer months. They believed Sirius added to the sun's heat, making those days hotter. Sirius

Name _____ Date _____

is the brightest star in the constellation Canis Major, or big dog. So, from Dog Star to dog days, the cliché came into being.

Writers sometimes use clichés to create a comic tone, appeal to a mass audience, or make readers feel comfortable. However, writers who want to say something in a fresh, new way should take this advice. Decide if the cliché will be understood by the reader. Check each time you're thinking about using a cliché. Finally, don't worry so much about using a cliché that you become dog-tired.

Now answer Numbers 30 through 35 on your Answer Sheet. Base your answers on the article "Clichés."

30 In which field did the term *cliché* originate?

F. clothing

G. mythology

H. pet ownership

I. printing

31 Read this dictionary entry.

> **stale** (steyl) *adjective*
> 1. dry or hardened from being kept too long
> 2. tasteless and flat
> 3. uninteresting from overuse
> 4. lacking in energy or ideas, as from boredom

Read this sentence from the article.

A cliché is a saying that is used so often it sounds stale and tired.

Which meaning best fits the way the word *stale* is used in the sentence above?

A. meaning 1

B. meaning 2

C. meaning 3

D. meaning 4

32 The cliché in the illustration is taken from

F. advice.

G. fashions.

H. human behavior.

I. weather.

33 Based on the article, the oldest cliché is most likely

A. gone to the dogs.

B. putting on the dog.

C. let sleeping dogs lie.

D. dog days of summer.

34 Which of the following best explains why the author selected dog clichés?

F. to show how common clichés are

G. to appeal to readers who own pets

H. to illustrate what most clichés are about

I. to convince readers to improve their writing

35 Read this sentence from the article.

> **Finally, don't worry so much about using a cliché that you become dog-tired.**

What does *dog-tired* mean in the sentence above?

A. anxious

B. annoyed

C. bored

D. exhausted

Name _____ Date _____

Revising and Editing

Read the introduction and the passage "Our Trip to the Wildflower Center" before answering Numbers 1 through 7.

Darlene wrote this passage about a trip she took with her class. Read her passage and think about the changes she should make.

Our Trip to the Wildflower Center

(1) Ms. Moore's fifth-grade class has been studying wildflowers that grow in Texas. (2) We went to the library to learn more about these flowers and where they grow in our state. (3) We learned that some flowers only grow in our state and do not grow anywhere else in the world. (4) Ms. Moore decided to finish the unit with a field trip to the Lady Bird Johnson Wildflower Center.

(5) Before boarding the school buses Ms. Moore assigned each of us both a partner, an observation journal. (6) We were a little late leaving the school, but we arrived at the center on time. (7) The first thing we did after getting off the bus was to work with our partneres to find a wildflower to observe and draw. (8) We also answered questions about its size, shape, color, and smell.

(9) A worker at the center taught us about the special features of the plants there. (10) Plants use these features to adapt to their environment. (11) Next, the worker led us on a hike. (12) He pointed out flowers with these features. (13) I noticed a roadrunner hiding in some grass. (14) "Wow you've got really sharp eyes!" the worker told me. (15) After the hike, we ate lunch at picnic tables that were surrounded by really, very nice wildflowers.

(16) Then, even though no one wanted to leave the center, it was time to go back to the school. (17) We asked our teacher if we could stay longer. (18) "Sorry" said Ms. Moore "we've got other subjects to study!" (19) Our class had enjoyed learning about wildflowers at the center. (20) The next day in class we shared our observations of the flowers.

Now answer Numbers 1 through 7 on your Answer Sheet. Base your answers on the changes Darlene should make.

1 Which sentence could best follow sentence 3?

A. You can buy wildflower seeds at a garden shop and grow your own.

B. Some students had never seen many of the flowers they learned about.

C. My aunt has a big vegetable garden, but she does not grow many flowers.

D. In the next unit, our class is going to learn about the native animals of Texas.

2 What is the best way to revise sentence 5?

F. Before boarding the school buses, Ms. Moore assigned each of us both a partner and an observation journal.

G. Before boarding the school buses. Ms. Moore assigned each of us both a partner and an observation journal.

H. Before boarding the school buses Ms. Moore assigned each of us both a partner or an observation journal.

I. Before boarding the school buses, Ms. Moore assigned each of us. Both a partner and an observation journal.

3 What change should be made in sentence 7?

    A. change *thing* to **things**

    B. change *did* to **done**

    C. change *partneres* to **partners**

    D. insert a comma after *wildflower*

4 What is the best way to revise sentences 11 and 12?

    F. Next, the worker led us on a hike and pointed out flowers with these features.

    G. Next, the worker led us and pointed out flowers with these features on a hike.

    H. Next, the worker led us on a hike. Then pointed out flowers with these features.

    I. Next, the worker led us on a hike that had flowers with these features pointed out.

5 What change should be made in sentence 14?

    A. insert a comma after *Wow*

    B. change *you've* to **youve**

    C. change *really* to **real**

    D. delete the quotation mark after *eyes!*

6 What change should be made in sentence 15?

    F. delete the comma after *hike*

    G. change *ate* to **eated**

    H. change *surround* to **surrounds**

    I. change *really, very nice* to **beautiful**

7 What is the best way to revise sentence 18?

A. "Sorry, said Ms. Moore "we've got other subjects to study!"

B. "Sorry said Ms. Moore we've got other subjects to study!"

C. "Sorry" said Ms. Moore "We've got other subjects to study!"

D. "Sorry!" said Ms. Moore. "We've got other subjects to study!"

Read the introduction and the article "A Healthful Snack" before answering Numbers 8 through 14.

Caleb has written an article for the school newspaper. Read his article and think about the changes he should make.

A Healthful Snack

(1) Children tend to eat a lot of snacks. (2) However, many of the snacks we eat are not good for us. (3) They contain too much fat or too much sugar, and some of them contain too much of both!

(4) I am going to tell you how to make a healthful snack at home. (5) It is not only quick and easy to make but it also tastes good and is fun to eat. (6) Most importantly, it is good for your health. (7) The snack is crunchy, raw vegetables served with dip.

(8) First, you will need to buy the ingredients needed to make the dip, as well as a variety of vegetables. (9) For the dip, you will need low-fat, plain yogurt and spices or seasonings that your family likes. (10) Ask an adult which spices or seasonings would be good to use. (11) For the vegetables, you can buy things such as carrots, celery, broccoli, and cauliflower.

(12) To begin, measure 2 cups of the yogurt, and put it in a bowl. (13) Next, measure 1 teaspoon each of the spices or seasonings that you choosed. (14) Be careful not to overdue the hot spices! (15) It will be too hot to eat. (16) If you add too much. (17) Stir these ingredients into the yogurt. (18) Ask an adult to help you cut the vegetables into bite-sized pieces.

(19) It is time to eat your tasty, healthful snack. (20) Dip the vegetable pieces into the yogurt dip. (21) The assortments of spices gives the dip its flavor. (22) You will be amazed at how too good it tastes!

Now answer Numbers 8 through 14 on your Answer Sheet. Base your answers on the changes Caleb should make.

8 What change should be made in sentence 5?

    F. insert a comma after *make*

    G. change *but* to **and**

    H. change *good* to **well**

    I. insert a comma after *fun*

9 What change should be made in sentence 13?

    A. change *Next* to **At last**

    B. change *measure* to **measuring**

    C. change *teaspoon* to **teaspoons**

    D. change *choosed* to **chose**

10 What change should be made in sentence 14?

    F. change *Be* to **Being**

    G. change *overdue* to **overdo**

    H. insert a comma after *hot*

    I. change the exclamation point to a question mark

11 What is the best way to combine sentences 15 and 16?

    A. It will be too hot to eat if you add too much.

    B. It will be too hot to eat or if you add too much.

    C. It will be too hot to eat but if you add too much.

    D. It will be too hot to eat and if you add too much.

Name _____ Date _____

12 What word or phrase could best be added to the beginning of sentence 19?

   F. However,

   G. Today,

   H. As a result,

   I. Finally,

13 What change should be made in sentence 21?

   A. change *assortments* to **assortment**

   B. insert a comma after *gives*

   C. change *dip* to **dips**

   D. change *flavor* to **flaver**

14 What change should be made in sentence 22?

   F. change *You* to **Your**

   G. change *amazed* to **amased**

   H. change *too good* to **delicious**

   I. change *tastes* to **taste**

Name _____ Date _____

Read the introduction and the article "Evening Classes" before answering Numbers 15 through 20.

Tyler wrote this article about an idea she has to improve her community. Read her article and think about the changes she should make.

Evening Classes

(1) I have an idea that I believe will help many people in our community.

(2) I think we should keep the schools open in the evenings so the people in

our community can participate in activities at them. (3) I know some taxpayers

are worried about the cost of keeping these schools open. (4) To them I will

say, "Sure but I believe the benefits will outweigh the drawbacks."

(5) Recently, I visited my cousin in Larchmont where the schools stay open

until 8:00 P.M. (6) Children and adults play sports in the school gyms and take

classes that are held in the library. (7) Children also take music lessens or get

extra help with reading. (8) Adults learn about computers and how to cook

foods from other countries, too. (9) People pay a small fee for each class but

the amount is very affordable. (10) The costs are low because volunteers teach

the classes.

(11) The more I learned about it, the more I thinked it would be good for

our community, too. (12) I believe these evening classes would be popular with

people of all ages. (13) We started this kind of program in our schools, people

would have fun learning new skills. (14) In addition, it would help bring our

community together. (15) Neighbors who were once strangers. (16) Would

become friends.

(17) Businesses in our community would also benefit. (18) Employees could take classes that would improve their work skills. (19) Young adults could take classes that teach the skills they'll need to get a job.

(20) I hope you will agree that there are many excellent reasons to keep the schools open in the evenings.

Now answer Numbers 15 through 20 on your Answer Sheet. Base your answers on the changes Tyler should make.

15 What change should be made in sentence 4?

    A. change *them* to **they**

    B. delete the comma after *say*

    C. insert a comma after *Sure*

    D. change *drawbacks* to **draw backs**

16 What change should be made in sentence 7?

    F. change *Children* to **Childrens**

    G. change *take* to **took**

    H. change *lessens* to **lessons**

    I. change *or* to a comma

17 What change should be made in sentence 9?

    A. change *People* to **Peoples**

    B. change *pay* to **paying**

    C. insert a comma after *class*

    D. change *amount* to **amownt**

18 What change should be made in sentence 11?

    F. delete the comma after *it*

    G. change *thinked* to **thought**

    H. change *be* to **being**

    I. change *our* to **ours**

19 Which word could best be added to the beginning of sentence 13?

    A. If

    B. Although

    C. Since

    D. Later

20 What revision is needed in sentences 15 and 16?

    F. Neighbors who were once strangers would become friends.

    G. Neighbors who were once. Strangers would become friends.

    H. Neighbors who were once strangers, and would become friends.

    I. Neighbors who were once strangers then they would become friends.

Name _____ Date _____

Writing Opinions

Read the prompt and plan your response.

Many people have an after-school activity that they enjoy.

Think about an after-school activity that you would like to see offered at your school.

Now write a persuasive essay to convince your principal to offer an after-school activity that you enjoy.

Planning Page

Use this space to make your notes before you begin writing. The writing on this page will NOT be scored.

_____

_____

_____

_____

_____

_____

_____

_____

_____

_____

_____

_____

_____

Name _____ Date _____

Begin writing your response here. The writing on this page and the next page WILL be scored.

_____

_____

_____

_____

_____

_____

_____

_____

_____

_____

_____

_____

_____

_____

_____

_____

_____

_____

_____

_____

_____

_____

_____

_____

_____

Name _____ Date _____

_____

_____

_____

_____

_____

_____

_____

_____

_____

_____

_____

_____

_____

_____

_____

_____

_____

_____

_____

_____

_____

_____

Reading Complex Text

Read the article "Guiding the Way to Freedom: Harriet Tubman and the Underground Railroad." As you read, stop and answer each question. Use evidence from the article to support your answers.

Guiding the Way to Freedom: Harriet Tubman and the Underground Railroad

A cloud slipped across the harvest moon. With the world below enveloped in darkness, six shadows left the cover of the trees. They entered a wide field, quickening their steps to keep up with their leader, a woman named Harriet Tubman. Despite her 4-foot, 11-inch stature, Tubman moved with the swiftness and sureness of a deer at home in these woods. The men and women in her party had heard stories about Harriet Tubman long before she arrived that Saturday night to guide them to freedom. Tubman had escaped to freedom several years before. Ever since then, this small, fearless woman had returned south time and again to lead other African American slaves to freedom.

In the years leading up to the Civil War, countless people risked their lives to help southern slaves find freedom in the North. Many did this through a secret network of routes leading into the North and eventually into Canada. This network came to be known as the Underground Railroad. Those who traveled with and guided escaped slaves were known as "conductors." Conductors and others dedicated to helping slaves escape knew of safe houses, or "stations," along the routes where groups could stop to rest and hide if needed. A woman named Harriet Tubman was one of the most famous, heroic conductors on the Underground Railroad.

1 What role did "conductors" and "stations" play in the Underground Railroad?

_____

_____

_____

Born as a slave in Maryland around 1820, Tubman grew up working on a large plantation. As early as six years old, Tubman's master sent her away from her parents to work as a house slave on another plantation. When she returned to her family, she was sent to work in the tobacco fields. To take her mind off the hard physical labor, Tubman listened as her fellow slaves told stories of others' attempts to escape.

Tubman resolved to one day run away and live as a free woman in the North. Tubman's father understood her spirit and determination better than anyone. Knowing how difficult the journey to freedom would be, Tubman's father taught her how to live in the woods. He also pointed out the North Star, explaining how to use it to navigate and find true north. In 1849, when she was 29 years old, Tubman learned that her master was planning to sell her to a plantation far away. The fateful moment had arrived. Tubman knew if she wanted to run away, she must act now.

❷ What does the word *navigate* mean as used in the section above?

_____

_____

_____

Ahead of them, Tubman paused in her tracks to scan the winter night sky. Spotting her guide, the gleaming North Star, she found north and forged ahead. Daylight was just hours away. By then, Tubman told them, they should reach the shop of a Maryland couple, stationmasters on the Underground Railroad. The couple had a secret shed where Tubman's party would be able to rest until nightfall Sunday. Then, the party would venture on. They would cross into Delaware, Tubman hoped, in the wee hours of Monday morning. Newspapers in Maryland would not print notices of runaway slaves until Monday morning. By that time, the group would be a long way from Maryland. The risk of being caught would be far lower.

THE UNDERGROUND RAILROAD

LEGEND
→ Routes of escape
Slave states in 1860
Free states in 1860

In 1849, under the dark cloak of night, Tubman began the first of what would be many journeys on the Underground Railroad. Leaving behind her husband, parents, and siblings, she traveled by night, following the Choptank River into Delaware. With the help of various people who offered her shelter and safety along the way, she eventually reached the free state of Pennsylvania. She had done it! Tubman's own freedom, however, was not enough. Soon after settling in Philadelphia, Tubman met a man named William Still. Still worked with the American Anti-Slavery Society and was active on the Underground Railroad. Tubman was determined to become a "conductor" and guide other slaves to freedom in the North.

Congress passed a new law in 1850, making it even more difficult for the Underground Railroad to operate. The first Fugitive Slave Act, passed in 1793, stated that escaped slaves must be returned to their owners. The Fugitive Slave Act of 1850 made it illegal to help runaway slaves. This meant that free states like Pennsylvania were no longer safe havens. Tubman would have to guide her "passengers" all the way to Canada. Between 1851 and 1860, Tubman made 19 trips between the South and the North. She helped lead over 300 slaves to freedom, including her sister and brothers' families and her own parents.

---

3   The map shows routes of escape on the Underground Railroad after 1850, when the Fugitive Slave Act was passed. How would this map have looked different before 1850?

_____

_____

_____

William Still once wrote of his friend and colleague, "The idea of being captured by slave-hunters or slave-holders seemed never to enter her mind. Harriet was supreme, and her followers generally had full faith in her, and would back up any word she might utter. It is probable [that someone like Tubman] was never known before or since."

"Weary from cold, miles of travel, and plain, raw fear, Tubman's Underground Railroad passengers pulled their heavy wool wraps tighter and trudged on. Once the journey had begun, there was no turning back. Her rule was law, but they knew this was for their own safety. If there was anyone they would trust with their lives, it was this courageous woman. Tubman was their own bright North Star, guiding their way to freedom.

Name _____ Date _____

4 What is one way the perspective in the italicized sections of the article is similar to the perspective in the sections of the article in regular print? What is one way the perspectives are different?

_____

_____

_____

_____

_____

Name _____ Date _____

Reading and Analyzing Text

Read the passage "In the News" and the newsletter "All the Neighborhood News" before answering Numbers 1 through 18.

In the News

"Hamilton, is your article finished yet?" Grady called as he looked through the papers on the floor. He was sorting the group's articles into piles. One pile had articles about the topic "Neat Stuff Our Neighbors Do"; another pile was for the topic "Neighborhood Happenings"; and the third pile was for Grady to sort later.

Hamilton brought another sheet of paper to Grady and said, "This article is current, so I think we should use it now." Grady put the article on the proper pile. Meanwhile, Jenna and Ava were working diligently at the computer. They were excited about the first issue of the group's new publication.

The friends had decided it would be fun if they wrote and produced a monthly newsletter for their neighborhood. They figured it would be a terrific way for people to learn about important neighborhood events, and it would also give everyone a new way to get to know each other a little better.

From a desk in the corner of the room, Maria reminded the staff, "We will launch the first issue on Friday, which means all articles must be submitted to Ava." She will position the articles in the design, and Jenna can make any necessary changes to the content so that it fits."

"I am sure we will meet our deadline!" Grady said, and everyone caught his enthusiasm.

On Saturday morning, all the neighbors found the result of the friends' hard work on their doorsteps.

Name _____ Date _____

All the Neighborhood News

Who Does What?

If you peek out your window around six o'clock in the morning, you might glimpse a curious sight. **Mr. Woodrow** might be in your front yard carrying a plastic bag! Do not be alarmed! He is just looking for old birds' nests that may have fallen during the night. Did you know he collects the nests and recycles them to make wonderful decorations? He crafts tiny scenes inside, often depicting birds doing human-like tasks. Ask to see his work, and you will want one for yourself!

Book enthusiast **Maddie McGwee** owns hundreds of children's books. At only age seven, she's well on her way to acquiring the largest collection of children's books in the neighborhood. She loves to read aloud to anyone who is willing to listen to a good story.

The next time you visit the home of **Dale and Donna Schmidt**, ask to see their new patio. As soon as you step onto their patio, you will feel like you are at a fiesta! They have built it in a style similar to something you might find in Mexico! You will love the bright colors, comfortable lawn chairs, and lively music they play. You can spend an hour looking at their collectibles and still not see everything. You will feel happy just being there! The butterflies seem to love it, too, as they flit from one bright pot of flowers to another.

Carol Starr is our local inventor! You might be wondering what that unusual piece of equipment is in her yard. We are, too! All we can report at this time is that Carol is working on a new invention. In the next issue, we'll let you know what she made and how it works.

The **Chang family** members all volunteer at the animal shelter every Sunday. They give regular workers some time off to be with their own families. They say that their volunteer work is more fun than anything else they do together. The animals love them and are always happy to see them. Luan, the youngest child in the family, says they make her laugh, and she loves to hear the kittens purr.

Who Needs Help?

Jason Hellerman is leading the drive to clean up the empty lot next to his family's house. Let's participate in this important activity on **Saturday, June 7**, so that children in our community will be able to use that area to play games. Remember to bring your work gloves and eye protection and to wear appropriate clothing. This is Jason's fourth project to help improve the neighborhood. In the fall, he will be starting the sixth grade. Consequently, we think he has a future as a group leader!

On the afternoon of June 22, **Mrs. Franklin** requires some help with polishing all her antique silverware, which is an enormous job! She promises to reward anyone who comes to help out with homemade lemonade and cookies.

Continued on next page

Name _____ Date _____

Who Needs Help *continued*

You might already know that **Mr. Madison** is moving. He will be packing up all his belongings next **Friday and Saturday, May 23 and 24**. We will miss him terribly, but he is looking forward to living closer to his relatives. If you can carefully wrap things and put them into boxes, he would welcome your assistance.

We hope you enjoyed this edition of our new neighborhood newsletter!

Let us know if you have some suggestions to make it better.

NOTE: *All the Neighborhood News* needs YOUR news! Please submit your ideas or happenings to Maria, Grady, Hamilton, Jenna, or Ava. Then be sure to read each edition, because you never know when YOUR name will appear in the news!

Now answer Numbers 1 through 18 on your Answer Sheet. Base your answers on the passage "In the News" and the newsletter "All the Neighborhood News."

 Read this dictionary entry.

---

current (KUR-uhnt) *adjective*

1. most recent

2. widespread; popular

3. publicly known

4. running; flowing

Read this sentence from the passage.

> **Hamilton brought another sheet of paper to Grady and said, "This article is current, so I think we should use it now."**

Which meaning best fits the way the word *current* is used in the sentence above?

A. meaning 1

B. meaning 2

C. meaning 3

D. meaning 4

Name _____ Date _____

2 Read this sentence from the passage.

> **They were excited about the first issue of the group's new publication.**

What does the word *publication* mean in the sentence above?

F. office

G. computer

H. printed work

I. article design

3 How does the third-person point of view of the passage influence how events are described?

A. Readers witness the making of the newsletter from Hamilton and Grady's perspectives.

B. Readers sense all of the friends' feelings and excitement as they work on the newsletter.

C. Readers must infer what each of the friends is thinking about as they put their articles together.

D. Readers experience the thoughts and reactions of all the neighbors as they read the newsletter.

4 Read this sentence from the passage.

> **The friends had decided it would be fun if they wrote and produced a monthly newsletter for their neighborhood.**

In the sentence above, the word *produced* means

F. created.

G. delivered.

H. found.

I. sold.

Name _____ Date _____

5 Read this sentence from the passage.

> **From a desk in the corner of the room, Maria reminded the staff, "We will launch the first issue on Friday, which means all articles must be submitted to Ava."**

What does the word *launch* mean in the sentence above?

A. make a start

B. jump forward

C. send into space

D. throw into the air

6 Read this sentence from the passage.

> **From a desk in the corner of the room, Maria reminded the staff, "We will launch the first issue on Friday, which means all articles must be submitted to Ava."**

Based on her words, what can the reader best conclude about Maria?

F. She is new to the group.

G. She is a leader in the group.

H. She has strong writing skills.

I. She writes most of the articles.

7 Read this sentence from the passage.

> **"We will launch the first issue on Friday, which means all articles must be submitted to Ava."**

Which word has the same base word as the word *submitted* in the sentence above?

A. mitten

B. submarine

C. submitting

D. summit

8 Why did the author position the passage "In the News" immediately before the newsletter "All the Neighborhood News"?

F. to show how the friends first came up with the idea for the newsletter

G. to show the relationships between the friends and their many neighbors

H. to show how the friends went about gathering the news for the newsletter

I. to show the work the friends did to put the neighborhood newsletter together

9 Why is the section *Who Does What*? important to the newsletter?

A. It persuades readers to start a book collection.

B. It tells a story about families that live together.

C. It gives interesting information about neighbors.

D. It criticizes people who live in the neighborhood.

10 Read this sentence from the newsletter.

> **Did you know he collects the nests and recycles them to make wonderful decorations?**

What does the word *recycles* mean in the sentence above?

F. uses again

G. already uses

H. does not use

I. uses too much

11 Read this sentence from the newsletter.

> **At only age seven, she's well on her way to acquiring the largest collection of children's books in the neighborhood.**

Which word has the same suffix as the word *largest* in the sentence above?

A. digest

B. houseguest

C. quickest

D. request

Name _____ Date _____

12 Read this sentence from the newsletter.

> **At only age seven, she's well on her way to acquiring the largest
> collection of children's books in the neighborhood.**

The word *acquiring* comes from the Latin root meaning

F. keep.

G. obtain.

H. read.

I. search.

13 Read this sentence from the newsletter.

> **As soon as you step onto their patio, you will feel like you are at
> a fiesta!**

Why does the author compare stepping onto the Schmidts' patio to attending
a fiesta?

A. to show the festive atmosphere of the Schmidts' patio

B. to illustrate activities that the Schmidts offer on their patio

C. to suggest that the Schmidts have frequently visited Mexico

D. to imply that the Schmidts have invited all of the neighbors to visit

14 Read this sentence from the newsletter.

> **You can spend an hour looking at their collectibles and still not
> see everything.**

What does the word *collectibles* mean in the sentence above?

F. someone who collects things

G. a place to display a collection

H. items that are worth collecting

I. a way of organizing a collection

Name _____ Date _____

15 Read this sentence from the newsletter.

> **All we can report at this time is that Carol is working on a
> new invention.**

Which of these shows the correct way to stress the syllables in the word
invention in the sentence above?

A. in • VEN • tion

B. in • ven • TION

C. IN • ven • tion

D. IN • ven • TION

16 Read this sentence from the newsletter.

> **Consequently, we think he has a future as a group leader!**

The Latin origin of the word *consequently* means

F. send forth.

G. turn around.

H. follow closely.

I. guide carefully.

17 Which of the following best describes the theme of the passage and newsletter?

A. Being informed about issues helps people make better decisions.

B. It is important for people to study and learn about different cultures.

C. Learning about one another is a good way to strengthen a community.

D. Not all team members contribute the same skills, but they contribute equally.

18 Why did the author write this passage and newsletter?

F. to show readers how newsletters are published

G. to describe a plan to improve the neighborhood

H. to persuade readers to write their own newsletters

I. to tell a story about children working together to reach a goal

Read the article "When You Grow Up" before answering Numbers 19 through 35.

When You Grow Up

What is your favorite activity or interest? Do you have any hobbies that you enjoy? When you become an adult, you might choose a career that matches one of your favorite things to do. Research shows that many people are happiest when they do work that they love.

If you spend a lot of time listening to music, you might enjoy being a disc jockey, or DJ. A DJ is the person who plays the songs you hear on the radio. A disc jockey may also interview famous guitar players or read the news on the radio show. Doing interviews can make this job very exciting. If you are interested in becoming a DJ, contact a local radio station. You might be able to work as a volunteer at the station and see real DJs at work. Later, you might go to broadcasting school to learn how to use the equipment that DJs use, how to interview people, and how to make use of other tricks of the trade.

Do you enjoy spending time outdoors away from big cities? As a park ranger, you could work outside much of the time. A park ranger's duties include caring for the wildlife that lives in the park, keeping park visitors safe, and monitoring the threat of forest fires and other hazards. It is extremely important and rewarding work. To learn more, contact your local park to see if you can shadow a ranger for a day. If you do decide to become a park ranger, you might go to a college or university to study wildlife and plants.

Maybe you feel a special connection with animals and want to help them. If so, you might love being a veterinarian. As a veterinarian, you would treat sick or injured animals. The best part is that you would not only be helping the animals, but also the animals' owners. They would be so grateful that you helped their pets! If you'd prefer to concentrate on working with wild animals, you could work in a zoo or a wildlife refuge. Whichever path you take, you will need to attend veterinary school.

Do you always want to find out what is happening in your community? You might think about a career as a journalist. Journalists often investigate important issues and current events. They can work for newspapers, magazines, web sites, or television stations. If your school has a newspaper or television station, contact the editor or manager and see if there are any opportunities for you to help. Later, you could study journalism at a college or university to learn how to ask questions to get the story and how to best deliver the information to your audience.

As you can see, your career choices are almost endless. Just about any interest can help you determine the job you will enjoy doing every day. Remember that in any job, you will need to know how to read, write, think clearly, and solve problems. For many of the jobs above, you will also need some formal education. If you master these skills and learn what is required, you will be all set to find a job that fits you like a glove.

Name _____ Date _____

If you are still undecided, don't worry. You still have plenty of time to figure out what you will do when you grow up.

Now answer Numbers 19 through 35 on your Answer Sheet. Base your answers on the article "When You Grow Up."

19 All of the following are main ideas included in the article EXCEPT

  A. there are a wide variety of career opportunities available.

  B. it is important to choose a career that best suit one's interests.

  C. previous paid work experience is important when choosing a career.

  D. skills, such as clear-thinking and problem-solving are important in any job.

20 Read this sentence from the article.

> **When you become an adult, you might choose a career that matches one of your favorite things to do.**

What does the word *career* mean in the sentence above?

  F. activity

  G. chore

  H. job

  I. worker

21 What idea does the author use to support the point that readers should choose a career based on their hobby or interest?

  A. By working as a volunteer, you can learn a lot about any job.

  B. For many jobs, you will need to go to a college or university.

  C. Research shows that people are happiest if they do work that they enjoy.

  D. You must know how to read, write, think clearly, and solve problems for any job.

Name _____ Date _____

22 Read this sentence from the article.

> **A disc jockey may also interview famous guitar players or read the news on the radio show.**

What does the word *guitar* mean in the sentence above?

F. a team sport

G. a recording of a song

H. a stringed musical instrument

I. a new kind of computer game

23 Read this dictionary entry.

> **trade** (trayd) *verb*
> **1.** to buy or sell
> **2.** to barter
> *noun*
> **3.** market
> **4.** business

Read this sentence from the article.

> **Later, you might go to broadcasting school to learn how to use the equipment that DJs use, how to interview people, and how to make use of other tricks of the trade.**

Which meaning best fits the way the word *trade* is used in the sentence above?

A. meaning 1

B. meaning 2

C. meaning 3

D. meaning 4

Name _____ Date _____

24 Which sentence from the article states a fact?

F. "If so, you might love being a veterinarian."

G. "It is extremely important and rewarding work."

H. "Doing interviews can make this job very exciting."

I. "A DJ is the person who plays the songs you hear on the radio."

25 Why does the author focus on describing four specific types of careers rather than giving a general overview of career choices?

A. The author wants to share information about careers unfamiliar to readers.

B. The author wants to describe careers that all readers would be interested in.

C. The author wants to show readers that careers can be based upon what they most enjoy doing.

D. The author wants to encourage readers to pursue careers that require college or university training.

26 Read this sentence from the article.

If you'd prefer to concentrate on working with wild animals, you could work in a zoo or a wildlife refuge.

What does the word *concentrate* mean in the sentence above?

F. draw

G. focus

H. search

I. think

27 In each paragraph that discusses a specific type of career, the author discusses

A. the benefits and drawbacks of the career.

B. the starting and ending salary for the career.

C. the duties and training that can be involved with the career.

D. the jobs and experiences that can help someone in that career.

28 Read this sentence from the article.

> **Journalists often investigate important issues and current events.**

What does the word *issues* mean in the sentence above?

F. countries

G. famous people

H. matters to discuss

I. helpful suggestions

29 Read this sentence from the article.

> **Journalists often investigate important issues and current events.**

Which word has the same base word as the word *investigate*?

A. gates

B. investigating

C. invading

D. vests

30 Read this sentence from the article.

> **They can work for newspapers, magazines, web sites, or television stations.**

What does the word *sites* mean in the sentence above?

F. grounds

G. installs

H. locates

I. pages

31 Read this sentence from the article.

> **As you can see, your career choices are almost endless.**

What does the word *endless* mean?

A. end again

B. ending soon

C. without end

D. too many ends

32 Read this sentence from the article.

> **If you master these skills and learn what is required, you will be all set to find a job that fits you like a glove.**

What does the author mean by the phrase *fits you like a glove*?

F. is perfect for you

G. is challenging for you

H. meets your expectations

I. prepares you for a career

33 Which sentence from the article states a fact?

A. "Do you always want to find out what is happening in your community?"

B. "They can work for newspapers, magazines, web sites, or television stations."

C. "If you spend a lot of time listening to music, you might enjoy being a disc jockey, or DJ."

D. "The best part is that you would not only be helping the animals, but also the animals' owners."

34 How does the author support the point that it is okay for readers to be undecided about a career?

    F. by explaining that changing careers can help readers decide on a career

    G. by giving tips about what readers can do to learn about different careers

    H. by explaining that there is still lots of time for readers to decide on a career

    I. by giving examples of people who were once undecided about their careers

35 Read this sentence from the article.

> **If you are still undecided, don't worry.**

What does the word *undecided* mean?

    A. decide again

    B. did not decide

    C. before deciding

    D. decide incorrectly

Revising and Editing

Read the introduction and the passage "Lonely Days" before answering Numbers 1 through 7.

Julie wrote this passage about getting a new journal. Read her passage and think about the changes she should make.

Lonely Days

(1) Gail, my best friend since the second grade, departed for summer camp two weeks ago. (2) When she informed me that she would be gone the entire summer, I was absolutely stuned. (3) I told her I was thrilled for her as I smiled bright, but inside I was unhappy. (4) How would I have any fun over the next couple of months?

(5) The next thing I learned was that my mother was departing to visit her younger sister, Aunt Mida, for 11 days. (6) Mom's absence meant a couple of things. (7) First, Dad would probably prepare his pancakes for dinner times several. (8) Pancakes were okay with me as long as he didn't insist on making them every night. (9) Second, I knew I would be lonely the majority of the time. (10) It wouldn't be easy to deal with this second circumstance.

(11) Anything seemed to tell my Mom that I had these negative feelings. (12) Before she left, she gave me a beautifully wrapped gift from Mr. Arnold's stationery store. (13) I opened the mysterious package and found a large, blue journal inside. (14) I wondered what I'd do with a book full of blank pages. (15) I discovered the answer soon after spending some time thinking for it. (16) When Mom finally got home, I showed her all the stuff and things I had written in my journal. (17) She hugged me and said, "Oh honey I knew you would know what to do with it!"

Now answer Numbers 1 through 7 on your Answer Sheet. Base your answers on the changes Julie should make.

1 What change should be made in sentence 2?

   A. change *informed* to **informing**

   B. change *me* to **I**

   C. insert a comma after *gone*

   D. change *stuned* to **stunned**

2 What change should be made in sentence 3?

   F. change *bright* to **brightly**

   G. change *but* to **however**

   H. change *was* to **will be**

   I. change *unhappy* to **inhappy**

3 What change should be made in sentence 7?

   A. change *Dad* to **dad**

   B. change *probably* to **probable**

   C. change *times several* to **several times**

   D. change the period to a question mark

4 What change should be made in sentence 11?

   F. change *Anything* to **Something**

   G. change *seemed* to **seem**

   H. change *that* to **which**

   I. change *these* to **this**

Name _____ Date _____

5 What change should be made in sentence 15?

   A. change *answer* to **anser**

   B. change *soon* to **sooner**

   C. change *spending* to **spent**

   D. change *for* to **about**

6 What change should be made in sentence 16?

   F. change *finally* to **final**

   G. change *got* to **comes back**

   H. change *stuff and things* to **poems and stories**

   I. change *written* to **wrote**

7 What is the best way to revise sentence 17?

   A. She hugged me and said "Oh honey I knew you would know what to do with it!"

   B. She hugged me and said, "Oh honey I knew you would know what to do with it"!

   C. She hugged me and said "Oh, honey I knew, you would know what to do with it!"

   D. She hugged me and said, "Oh, honey, I knew you would know what to do with it!"

Read the introduction and the passage "Lynette's First Pony" before answering Numbers 8 through 14.

Sharlene wrote this passage about a girl who gets a pony. Read her passage and think about the changes she should make.

Lynette's First Pony

(1) When she was seven years old, Lynette acquired her first pony. (2) It was a great surprise, and it took her breath away. (3) It was exciting for the whole family, too, and watching her enjoymant made all of them absolutely delighted.

(4) Dad had taken Lynette to see dozens of ponies, but none of them was suitable until she spotted Rascal. (5) Then it was love at first sight! (6) Rascal was different amounts of colors, which made him very cute. (7) The little pony was also stubborn, but he was definitely no match for Lynette.

(8) With the owner's permission, Lynette took Rascal for a ride. (9) First, she put on her helmet, and with Dad's help she placed a saddle and reins on Rascal. (10) Then Lynette climbed at the pony and rode him around the corral. (11) Rascal's owner looked on in amazement and told Lynette that he had never seen everyone else ride Rascal so easily.

(12) Lynette rode Rascal every chance she got. (13) In the summer, she would ride him from sunup until sundown. (14) Her grandparents lived on a farm across the road from her house. (15) Lynette covered every square inch

of their land hundreds of times. (16) She never grew tired of riding or the view

beautiful from Rascal's back.

(17) As of today Lynette has graduated to riding a larger horse, but she still

hasn't forgotten Rascal. (18) Lynette always takes the pony a carrot or an apple

chunk before she rides her new horse. (19) She is also teaching a neighbor

boy how to ride on Rascal. (20) The pony is a little older and he moves more

slowest now, but he's still stubborn. (21) He's still no match for Lynette!

Now answer Numbers 8 through 14 on your Answer Sheet. Base your answers on the changes Sharlene should make.

8 What change should be made in sentence 3?

    F. change *exciting* to **excited**

    G. change *her* to **she**

    H. change *enjoymant* to **enjoyment**

    I. change *delighted* to **delited**

9 What change should be made in sentence 6?

    A. change *different amounts of colors* to **brown and tan with white spots**

    B. change *which* to **what**

    C. change *made* to **making**

    D. change *cute* to **cuteness**

10 What change should be made in sentence 10?

    F. change *Then* to **Than**

    G. change *climbed* to **climb**

    H. change *at* to **on**

    I. insert a comma after *pony*

11 What change should be made in sentence 11?

    A. change the comma to a period

    B. change *told* to **tells**

    C. change *never* to **not ever**

    D. change *everyone* to **anyone**

12 What change should be made in sentence 16?

    F. change *She* to **She'll**

    G. change *grew* to **grow**

    H. change *of* to **on**

    I. change *view beautiful* to **beautiful view**

13 What change should be made in sentence 17?

    A. insert comma after *today*

    B. change *graduated* to **graduation**

    C. change *larger* to **largest**

    D. change *hasn't* to **has'nt**

14 What change should be made in sentence 20?

    F. insert a comma after *older*

    G. change *slowest* to **slowly**

    H. change *he's* to **he'd**

    I. change *stubborn* to **stubbornly**

Read the introduction and the passage "New Kid on the Block" before answering Numbers 15 through 20.

Greg has written a passage about a boy who meets a new neighbor. Read his passage and think about the changes he should make.

New Kid on the Block

(1) Jeremy stood on the corner and gloomily observed a moving van stop on front of an empty house. (2) Yesterday Kyle Noland, his best friend, had lived there, but today Kyle was gone. (3) It seemed to Jeremy that it had happened overnight.

(4) In fact, the Nolands had been planning to move for several months, ever since Mrs. Noland received a fabulous new job offer in another state. (5) Kyle was not happy that they were moving, but he realized that the move was best for his whole family. (6) Of course, Jeremy and him vowed to e-mail each other and stay in touch.

(7) Jeremy stared at the ground, not really focused on anything, remembering the fun times that he and Kyle had had together. (8) That was why he did not notice a girl standing next to him. (9) "So what's this neighborhood like?" she asked, waking Jeremy from his daydream.

(10) "This place is very, very good," Jeremy responded, shaking himself out of his fog.

(11) "Great!" the girl exclaimed. (12) Then she pointed to Kyle's former home and said, "My name is Samantha. (13) I'm moving into that house, so I hope there are some kids who are fun in this neighborhood. (14) Are you one of them?"

(15) Jeremy smiled and said, "Absolutely! (16) Are YOU fun?"

(17) That made Samantha laugh. (18) "I'll try to be," she joked.

(19) Jeremy liked her right away and appreciated her sense of humor.

(20) He immediately decided that she might be a really, really nice addition to the neighborhood. (21) He offered to introduce her to the other kids who lived on their street, so they strolled up and down the street and chatted with anyone who was outdoors. (22) They finally ended up in front of Samantha's new house. (23) "See you around," she said, waving goodbye.

Now answer Numbers 15 through 20 on your Answer Sheet. Base your answers on the changes Greg should make.

15 What change should be made in sentence 1?

   A. change *and* to **while**

   B. change *gloomily* to **gloomy**

   C. change *observed* to **observe**

   D. change *on* to **in**

16 What change should be made in sentence 6?

   F. change *him* to **he**

   G. change *each* to **the**

   H. change *stay* to **staye**

   I. change the period to a question mark

17 What change should be made in sentence 9?

    A. insert a comma after *So*

    B. change the question mark to a comma

    C. insert a period after *asked*

    D. change *waking* to **woke**

18 What change should be made in sentence 10?

    F. change *This* to **These**

    G. change *very, very good* to **fantastic**

    H. change *responded* to **responding**

    I. change *himself* to **his self**

19 What change should be made in sentence 13?

    A. change *so* to **since**

    B. change *there* to **their**

    C. change *kids who are fun* to **fun kids**

    D. change *this* to **those**

20 What change should be made in sentence 20?

    F. insert a comma after *immediately*

    G. change *she* to **she's**

    H. change *really, really nice* to **terrific**

    I. change *addition* to **addishun**

Name _____ Date _____

Writing to Narrate

Read the prompt and plan your response.

Most people have planned or attended a celebration.

Think about a time you planned or attended a celebration.

Now write a personal narrative about a time you planned or attended a celebration.

Planning Page

Use this space to make your notes before you begin writing. The writing on this page will NOT be scored.

_____

_____

_____

_____

_____

_____

_____

_____

_____

_____

_____

_____

Name _____ Date _____

Begin writing your response here. The writing on this page and the next page WILL be scored.

_____
_____
_____
_____
_____
_____
_____
_____
_____
_____
_____
_____
_____
_____
_____
_____
_____
_____
_____
_____
_____
_____
_____
_____
_____

Name _____ Date _____

_____

_____

_____

_____

_____

_____

_____

_____

_____

_____

_____

_____

_____

_____

_____

_____

_____

_____

_____

_____

_____

_____

Name _____ Date _____

Reading Complex Text

Read the articles "A Balancing Act" and "Father Extraordinaire." As you read, stop
and answer each question. Use evidence from the articles to support your answers.

A Balancing Act

An icy wind whips across the frozen sea ice off the coast of Antarctica. It is June, and
the temperature has dipped to –40 degrees Fahrenheit. Winter in Antarctica has begun. A
group of male emperor penguins huddles together in a tight formation to protect themselves
from the harsh winds. But that is not all they are protecting. Tucked under a thick fold of
skin, called a brood pouch, each of these male penguins balances an egg on its feet, keeping
it warm and protecting it from the ice. This is where the egg will remain, cozy and safe,
until it hatches in two months.

Compared to many other males in the animal kingdom, the male emperor penguin plays
a unique and special role in caring for its young. Where, you might ask, is the female during
this time? If you think the mother penguin is touring the globe or sunning herself in a
warmer climate, think again! After laying her egg in late spring, the female promptly heads
for the sea to hunt. Her journey can be up to 50 miles long. She spends the next two months
hunting fish, squid, and krill. She eats as much as she can before finding her way back to her
partner—and her newly-hatched chick.

1 How does the male emperor penguin's role in caring for the egg differ from the
female's role?

_____

_____

_____

While the female emperor penguin is busy feeding, the male must tend to the egg. With
the eggs balanced on their feet, the males huddle together for warmth. They don't stay put,
however. The entire mass of penguins shuffles along the ice, each penguin taking tiny steps
forward in the same direction. Scientists have studied this fascinating behavior. They have
found that, together, the penguins actually create a wave-like movement. As new penguins
join the group, the other male penguins move forward several inches. This allows them to
remain closely packed. It also gives every penguin the chance to spend time on both the
inside of the huddle, where it is warmest, and on the outskirts, where it is coldest.

Name _____ Date _____

One August day, the male's careful, hard work pays off, though his job is far from over. The egg hatches, and a fuzzy, gray chick appears! Still too young to survive on its own, the chick stays cozy in its father's brood pouch. The father must provide food for his young until the mother returns. He produces a milk-like substance from a pouch in his throat and feeds the chick.

Nature's timing is perfect. Just as the father is about to run out of food for the chick, the mother returns to the colony. She is welcomed by her partner (who is undoubtedly ready for a gigantic meal!) and her new chick. After her several-month-long feeding expedition, the mother has a belly full of food. She regurgitates, or spits up, some of this food for her chick. Now, it is time for the male and female to swap places. The male heads for the ocean to hunt, and the female takes over the care of her chick, keeping it warm and safe in her own brood pouch. When summer arrives in January, the young chick will finally be able to fend for itself. Until then, it is lucky to have two dependable parents to rely upon in this vast, icy Antarctic home.

---

2 What evidence does the author give to support the idea that "nature's timing is perfect"?

_____

_____

_____

Father Extraordinaire

Blades of sea grass flutter back and forth in the warm, shallow ocean water. This movement catches the eye of a scuba diver exploring the ocean floor. The diver propels herself forward for a closer look. She discovers that it is not the current that is causing this sea grass to "dance." Dozens of baby sea horses are clutching onto the plants' blades with their monkey-like tails! These babies made their entrance into the watery world just twelve hours ago. They have been on their own since the moment of birth. The story of the sea horses' birth and the days leading up to it is quite remarkable. The father sea horse plays a very important role in this story.

Unlike the behavior of mammals, it is not unusual for female fish to lay their eggs and then swim off. It is also not unusual for male fish to look after the eggs. Among sea horses, however, the father's role is especially unique. Much like a female kangaroo, the male sea horse has a pouch, called a brood pouch, on the front of his body. The female sea horse leaves her eggs in this pouch. After that, the mother's job is over. For the next two to seven weeks, it is the male who dutifully carries the eggs. His sealed pouch is the lifeline for his growing young, providing food and oxygen.

3 What is one way in which sea horse fathers and penguin fathers are alike?

_____

_____

_____

Finally, the eggs are ready to hatch. The father sea horse's pouch opens, and the baby sea horses swim out one by one. Some of the babies use their tails to grasp onto the father in those first minutes of life. Others grasp each other. Most of them wriggle away, fully prepared to survive on their own.

---

4 How does the author organize the information in each article?

_____

_____

_____

_____

Name _____ Date _____

Reading and Analyzing Text

Read the passages "A New Fan" and "Bon Appétit" before answering Numbers 1 through 7.

A New Fan

"But *Mom!*" Susie Chang knew her mother hated it whenever she whined, but she continued anyway.

"Honey," said Susie's mother, stretching her lips across her teeth as she applied a coat of Blushing Burgundy lipstick, "don't you have some guests to attend to?"

"We're making bracelets and anklets, and they're fine."

"That's wonderful. How do I look?" Susie's mother, dressed in a shimmering emerald green evening gown, struck a model's pose.

"Like a traitor," Susie pouted. "When I organized this slumber party, you said you were going to be home." At the last minute, Susie's mother had been invited to host an important charity function in the city with her dad.

"We won't be getting home all that late. And don't worry. Nai Nai will be right here all evening long."

Susie's face darkened visibly. Not one of her friends referred to their grandmother as *Nai Nai*, and none of them had a grandmother who lived with them either. Susie's grandmother had moved into the house about six months ago from Minneapolis, where she had lived with Susie's Ye Ye, or Grandpa Joe. When Ye Ye died, Nai Nai had relocated and was now living with Susie's family. Though Susie hardly knew her, she was confident that no one else had a grandmother quite like Nai Nai.

After her mother's elegant departure, Susie rejoined her company downstairs in the living room, where they were twisting embroidery threads into colorful bracelets, anklets, and other accessories. Nai Nai was sitting in the corner, playing a game of solitaire in the glow of a fringed floor lamp, with a delicate pair of half-moon spectacles sitting primly on the bridge of her nose.

"I sure wish my grandma would, like, go to the veranda, or something," Susie muttered under her breath to Anna, whom she'd known since kindergarten.

Shocked, Anna turned to look at Nai Nai. "Why?"

"Talk about invading my personal space." Susie stole a glance at the corner. Nai Nai was wearing one of those dresses made of a shiny satin fabric that fastened at the neck. Why couldn't she just wear jeans, or a tracksuit, like any normal grandmother?

"Chill out, Susie," said Hillary, whom Susie had met the year before playing youth basketball. "It's 90 degrees outside—just enjoy the air conditioning."

Nai Nai nodded at Susie then abruptly frowned in the direction of the sofa. "Not feeling so good?"

Susie turned to see Greta, her best friend, lying across half the couch, holding a cushion to her forehead. "It's just a really bad headache," moaned Greta. "And it's my own fault—I was reading without my glasses."

Without a word, Nai Nai scurried to the kitchen, quickly returning with a cup of steaming liquid. "Herbal tea," said Nai Nai. "It has hibiscus blossom and honey. It's good for treating a headache," she explained, sitting next to Greta. And then, the lights went out.

With a single voice, everyone screamed. Anna yelled, "Flashlights!"

"They're in the kitchen!" said Susie, fumbling her way to the adjoining room. "Oh, I can't believe it—this is the unluckiest slumber party ever!" Her friends were stumbling along behind her, each girl holding on to the one in front, like boxcars in a railroad train.

"No, it's not," giggled Greta. "It's awesome!"

Susie peered out the kitchen window, noticing that her neighbors' homes—and the streetlights—had also gone dark. "The power's gone out on the entire street—super. Here, have a flashlight."

"You call these flashlights?" Anna laughed. Two puny beams of light struggled to penetrate the blackness.

"You know what's worse than no light?" Becca asked through the darkness. "No air conditioning!"

The girls all groaned their agreement. Then a sound made them swivel around and gaze toward the fireplace at the back of the room. On the mantle, a little flame appeared, then another and another, until a row of light danced across the mantle. Nai Nai had set up the candles and lit them one by one.

"Oooh," the girls marveled in unison. They moved toward the fireplace as if drawn by an unseen magnet. Then they arranged themselves around the hearth and admired the flickering lights.

"My candle collection was packed away," said Nai Nai. "Now we get to put it to good use." She picked up a slender candle and used it to help light her way out of the living room.

"Your grandmother is so awesome," said Hillary.

"And so is this party!" Julie added. "Hey, you know, I bet if we stay really still, we won't be so hot." As if on cue, Nai Nai returned and began passing out small solid objects from a bulky plastic bag. Initially confused, the girls examined the items in the flickering light.

"I know!" Greta yelled. With a flap, she shook open what was suddenly a semi-circular fan. Nai Nai had handed one to each girl. As the girls batted the fans at themselves and each other, they admired the patterns painted on them—cypress trees, cherry blossoms, and buffaloes.

As she waved her fan, Susie's tension let go in the comforting atmosphere of the candlelight. It was funny how here, in the darkness, she could see Nai Nai more clearly than ever before.

Bon Appétit!

"How long was I supposed to let the pasta cook?" I mumbled to myself, as I gave the marinara sauce a quick stir with the wooden spoon and peeked under the lid of the steamer to see if the green beans looked ready. They did: far, far too ready. In fact, they resembled limp, olive-colored shoe laces more than the bright, crisp green vegetables I had been aiming for. There was no time to despair though. Just as I seized a pair of oven mitts and lifted the steamer into the sink to cool, the pasta water rose up and spilled over the lip of the pot, hissing at me as it hit the stovetop. Quickly, I turned the burner off and seized the pot in my oven mitts. So far, cooking a meal for my family had been one massive juggling act, and I felt like I was dropping balls right and left. I sighed. At least my marinara sauce, made from scratch and bubbling gently in the saucepan, looked more than edible—perfect even—just as I had hoped. It better be perfect, I thought, after I had spent all afternoon chopping onions, basil leaves and garlic—so much garlic.

The kitchen door swung open, and my older sister Sara waltzed in. "Okay, Evan, the table is all set, Gran and Grandpa are here, and everyone is just sitting down at the table. Is there anything else I can do to help?" she asked.

I was still standing and holding the pot in my oven mitts. "Um, I forgot to put a colander in the sink to drain the pasta water. Can you grab one?"

"Of course," Sara agreed. "And then I'll just carry the beans out to the table, okay?"

"Thanks," I said, heaving a sigh of relief. "I'll be right behind you with the pasta and marinara sauce."

A few minutes later, I was proudly ladling piping-hot red sauce over heaps of penne pasta on my family members' dinner plates. Overcooked beans aside, I couldn't wait for everyone to taste my homemade tomato sauce. "Evan, you have outdone yourself, truly," Gran exclaimed. "This looks wonderful!" she said, as I passed her a full, steaming plate.

"It smells very garlicky, not to mention delicious!" my mom said.

"Well, garlic is one of the main ingredients in the sauce," I replied, and then I announced proudly, "Bon appétit, everyone!"

Instead of digging into my own dish, I watched my family dig into theirs. Even though cooking the meal had been a hectic experience, it was the moment when everyone praised the perfection of my sauce that I had been imagining all day.

Grandpa reacted first, just not in the way I had expected. "Uhh-UM," he gargled, barely managing to swallow his mouthful of pasta. From across the table, Sara looked as though she had bit into a lemon.

Name _____ Date _____

"Oh no! What's the matter?" I groaned.

"Um, Evan, how much garlic did the sauce recipe call for?" Mom asked gently.

"Three to four cloves," I replied. I was totally confused; I had followed the recipe exactly.

"Evan, is there a chance you might have used three bulbs of garlic instead of just three small cloves?" Dad asked.

"You mean . . . a bulb of garlic is made up of many cloves, and I was just supposed to use three of those smaller pieces?" I didn't even need to phrase it as a question. As soon as the words tumbled out of my mouth, I knew the answer. I buried my face in my hands, mumbling, "I'm so sorry, everyone. I just wanted this meal to be perfect."

"Honey," my mom said, "I know how disappointed and embarrassed you are, but the look on your Grandpa's face . . ." she giggled. "Did I ever tell you about the time I was making a new beef recipe called 'Coffee Roast'? The recipe called for one cup of coffee. So I opened a bag of coffee beans, ground up a cup's worth, poured the fresh grounds all over that roast, and stuck it in the oven. Suffice to say, your dad and I were picking coffee grounds out of our teeth for days."

Despite my misery, I couldn't help but join my family in laughing—Mom laughing harder than any of us.

"The first time I made a pot of chili," Grandpa boomed, "I didn't know there was a difference between chili powder and cayenne pepper. Well, there is. I dumped loads of cayenne pepper into that pot of chili, and as a result, we were breathing fire for days. It was so spicy, we had to toss it out."

Everyone burst out laughing again, me included. "Evan," my sister said, "I'm sure next time you make this recipe, it will turn out great. Experience is the best teacher, you know. And I promise that, one of these days, you'll laugh harder than anyone when you share this story over someone else's cooking disaster."

I grinned sheepishly, pushed my plate forward, and stood up. "For now, though, I'm going to go order us a pizza!"

Now answer Numbers 1 through 7 on your Answer Sheet. Base your answers on the passages "A New Fan" and "Bon Appétit."

1 Read this sentence from the passage "A New Fan."

> **"I sure wish my grandma would, like, go to the veranda, or something," Susie muttered under her breath to Anna, whom she'd known since kindergarten.**

What does the sentence above best reveal about Susie's character?

A. She is angry at Nai Nai.

B. She is embarrassed by Nai Nai.

C. She enjoys Nai Nai's company.

D. She and Nai Nai are not getting along.

2 Read this excerpt from the passage "A New Fan."

> **"Herbal tea," said Nai Nai. "It has hibiscus blossom and honey. It's good for treating a headache," she explained, sitting next to Greta.**

The excerpt above reveals that Nai Nai most likely

F. grows hibiscus in her backyard.

G. enjoys drinking many kinds of tea.

H. does not believe in traditional medicine.

I. has experience treating headaches with tea.

3 Read this sentence from the passage "A New Fan."

> **It was funny how here, in the darkness, she could see Nai Nai more clearly than ever before.**

The author ends the passage with the sentence above in order to show that the conflict within Susie

A. will continue until her mother returns home.

B. is resolved as she comes to appreciate Nai Nai.

C. will continue until Nai Nai leaves her and her friends alone.

D. is resolved as her friends help distract her from her thoughts.

Name _____ Date _____

4 Read this sentence from the passage "Bon Appétit."

> **So far, cooking a meal for my family had been one massive juggling act, and I felt like I was dropping balls right and left.**

Why does the author compare Evan's cooking experience to a juggling act?

F. to show that Evan wishes he had chosen a different recipe

G. to show that Evan keeps dropping things on the floor as he cooks

H. to show that Evan finds it hard to handle all the cooking tasks at once

I. to show that Evan isn't having as much fun cooking as he thought he would

5 Read this excerpt from the passage "Bon Appétit."

> **"Evan," my sister said, "I'm sure next time you make this recipe, it will turn out great. Experience is the best teacher, you know."**

What is meant by the saying *Experience is the best teacher* in the sentence above?

A. Some experiences should best be forgotten.

B. It is good to try and pursue new experiences.

C. Sometimes lack of experience can get you into trouble.

D. Some things are best learned from practical experience.

6 Which of the following best tells how the points of view of the passage "A New Fan" and "Bon Appétit" are different?

F. "A New Fan" is told by an unconcerned observer.

G. "Bon Appétit" is narrated by the grandparents.

H. In "A New Fan," the narrator is also the main character.

I. In "Bon Appétit," the narrator is also the main character.

7 In both passages, "A New Fan" and "Bon Appétit," the main characters learn that

A. first impressions are not always right.

B. they should learn to trust other people.

C. things don't always go according to plan.

D. it is important to be able to laugh at oneself.

Read the article "Steven Bishop: Cave Explorer" before answering Numbers 8 through 13.

Stephen Bishop: Cave Explorer

by Judith Boogaart

At Mammoth Cave in Kentucky, Stephen Bishop was known as the "prince of guides."

Stephen gained his freedom in 1856, but died the following year. His body lies in the Old Guides Cemetery near the cave he loved.

Stephen's lantern cast shaky shadows on the walls of Mammoth Cave, Kentucky. Hurrying after his guide, he stumbled along the rocky path. He couldn't lose sight of Mr. Miller. He might not find his way back out.

Stephen was a slave owned by Franklin Gorin. Gorin had bought Mammoth Cave to develop it for tourists. Like many people in the 1830s, he didn't worry about preserving the natural wonder. He wanted to make money from it. Since a slave wouldn't need to be paid, Gorin decided to have 17-year-old Stephen trained as a guide.

Facing the Challenge

Stephen knew little about caves, but he was expected to obey his master. Every day, he followed his guide, Mr. Miller, over the cave routes. Stephen found he could easily remember the twisting passages and the formations that served as markers. Soon he knew the eight miles of cave routes as well as Mr. Miller.

But guiding meant more than knowing the trails. Stephen had to explain what visitors were seeing. He listened closely to learn facts and stories about the caves.

Name _____ Date _____

This passage is called Cleaveland Avenue.

Soon Stephen began giving tours himself. He pointed out log pipes and wooden vats in the passages. These had been used in the mining of saltpeter to make gunpowder for the War of 1812.

He took visitors deep underground to Chief City. Here, early tribes had left behind slippers, gourds, and cane sticks. Stephen lit fires to show off the room's huge size.

In Registration Hall, miners, guides, and visitors had used smoke from lamps or candles to write their names on the smooth ceiling. Legend says Stephen learned to read and write by studying them. Soon he added his name to theirs.

Exploring Mammoth Cave

Stephen loved the cave. While giving tours, he spotted many leads off the main passages. He itched to explore them, and Gorin let him. More passages meant more cave tours—and more money for Gorin.

Stephen spent hours underground. He climbed up domes and down pits. In the dim light of his tin lamp, he squeezed through narrow tunnels and crawl spaces. He memorized landmarks such as special rocks or sand beds to guide himself back out.

One day, Stephen followed a twisting passage not on the tours. He climbed up a slick wall, over slopes, and down a 30-foot drop. He crawled through an opening partway up the passage wall. There he found a large dome no one had known about. Gorin was thrilled. It was named Gorin's Dome, and newspapers printed stories of the discovery.

Beyond Bottomless Pit

Stephen kept exploring, but one space always stopped him: Bottomless Pit. On tours, he lit scraps of paper and tossed them in. Visitors, watching them drift down, could never see the bottom. The pit gaped as wide as a country lane. No one had ever dared to cross it. But Stephen wanted to know what was on the other side.

On October 20, 1838, Stephen and a visitor decided to risk it. Using a ladder of cedar poles, they crossed over Bottomless Pit. Imagine inching over a yawning black hole on a crude ladder. "I'm not sure I would have tried it," admits Chuck DeCroix, an experienced caver who guides visitors today. "They had poor lighting and no knowledge of what was below them. It would take guts to cross."

Stephen's courage paid off. He and the visitor found two miles of new passages that day. What beautiful stalactites, stalagmites, and gypsum rosettes they saw! Again Gorin was thrilled. He had a sturdy bridge built across the pit. Guides and visitors explored six more miles of passages that year.

159

Stephen discovered underground rivers in Mammoth Cave. He saw eyeless fish swimming in them. No one had heard of such creatures. Scientists came from all over the world to study them.

Eyeless fish swim in the Cave's rivers.

Stephen became famous for his dramatic tours. He gave boat trips on the rivers. He showed off a beautiful place called Snowball Room. Its ceiling was covered with white gypsum rosettes. He used lantern light and torches to make formations sparkle and glow. He sang songs to demonstrate the cave's great sound. He told interesting stories. One visitor called him the "prince of guides."

Stephen drew a new map of Mammoth Cave. Slaves didn't usually get credit for their accomplishments, but the map was published in 1845 under Stephen's name.

For 150 years, other people have continued to explore the cave. Today, 365 miles have been surveyed in the Mammoth Cave system. It is the longest cave in the world. Stephen Bishop found more miles of passage than any other guide of his time. His curiosity, determination, and courage helped him discover Mammoth's secrets.

Thousands of *spelunkers*, amateur cave explorers, take guided tours of Mammoth Cave each year. Only experienced cavers explore and survey new passages.

Six Spelunking Safety Rules

1. Get permission first.
2. Use the right equipment.
3. Tell two people your plans.
4. Take three lights each.
5. Take at least four people.
6. If lost or without light, stay put!

Name _____ Date _____

Now answer Numbers 8 through 13 on your Answer Sheet. Base your answers on the article "Steven Bishop: Cave Explorer."

8 The photographs in the article help readers understand

    F. how the cave's owner, Gorin, made money from Mammoth Cave.

    G. some of the early methods Bishop used to explore Mammoth Cave.

    H. some of the things Bishop discovered as he explored Mammoth Cave.

    I. how Mammoth Cave would have looked when Bishop first explored it.

9 Which of these details from the article states an opinion about Bishop?

    A. He made money for the cave's owner.

    B. He found many miles of cave passages.

    C. He was considered the prince of guides.

    D. He discovered eyeless fish in the cave's rivers.

10 Read this dictionary entry.

lead (leed) *noun*
1. the first or foremost place
2. a leash
3. a piece of information that helps guide; a tip or clue
4. a guide or indication of a road or course

Read this sentence from the article.

While giving tours, he spotted many leads off the main passages.

Which meaning best fits the way the word *leads* is used in the sentence above?

    F. meaning 1

    G. meaning 2

    H. meaning 3

    I. meaning 4

Name _____ Date _____

11 Read this sentence from the article.

Imagine inching over a yawning black hole on a crude ladder.

How would the effect of this sentence be different if the author had used the word *going* instead of *inching*?

A. It would make the act seem less fun.

B. It would make the act seem more difficult.

C. It would make the act seem less terrifying.

D. It would make the act seem more dangerous.

12 Stephen Bishop made his map of Mammoth Cave

F. after he received his freedom.

G. before he learned to read and write.

H. before he crossed the Bottomless Pit.

I. after he discovered the underground rivers.

13 All of the following are main ideas of the article EXCEPT

A. Bishop put lots of time and effort into learning cave routes.

B. Bishop made many important discoveries inside Mammoth Cave.

C. Bishop courageously explored many new passages inside Mammoth Cave.

D. Bishop was only 17 when Franklin Gorin decided to have him trained as a guide.

162

Read the article "The Ellis Island Experience" before answering Numbers 14 through 18.

The Ellis Island Experience

Ellis Island lies in New York Harbor, with a view of the Statue of Liberty and New York City's impressive skyline. Between 1892 and 1954, over twelve million immigrants entered the United States through Ellis Island.

Before they arrived in New York Harbor, immigrants had already made tough decisions. Some decided to leave behind family and friends, perhaps never to see them again, while others sold everything they couldn't carry to pay for their tickets. Most made the long sea trip beneath the deck in cramped conditions. Immigrants often traveled with the cargo and were included on the ship's cargo list, along with barrels of food and bolts of wool. Immigrants put up with all of this in order to seek out fresh opportunities in a new world.

When they arrived at Ellis Island, all immigrants had one question: Could they begin new lives in the United States, or would they have to get back on a ship and return home? Happiness, hope, and sometimes heartbreak filled the station's rooms as each immigrant waited for the answer to this question. Most made it through the tests; about two percent had to return home.

In the Harbor

Before any ship could dock in New York City, inspectors came on board and checked passengers for any contagious[1] illness. Passengers who were ill had to be treated before being allowed to go ashore. Once cleared, first and second class passengers got on a ferry to the city, and then the other passengers from the ship came up on deck, dragging suitcases and trunks heavy with everything they owned. Each person and piece of baggage was tagged with a piece of paper giving the name of the ship and their number on the cargo list. Then the newcomers took a ferry to the Ellis Island station.

In the Baggage Room

At Ellis Island, immigrants were instructed to place their baggage in a pile to spare them from having to drag it through the station during the arrival process. However, some immigrants refused. They feared their baggage—everything they had brought to the new country—would be lost or stolen.

[1] **contagious:** spreads from person to person

With or without their suitcases, immigrants formed a line and walked up the broad stairs to the Registry Room. As they walked, doctors and inspectors checked them again for illness or other medical problems. Doctors looked at each person's scalp, face, neck, hands, and way of walking. Doctors asked people to remove their hats and unbutton their high collars. This way, doctors could check for problems more easily. Some immigrants found the exam embarrassing. Whenever doctors saw a problem, they took chalk and wrote a code on the person's clothing.

Other doctors checked each person for signs of contagious illness. Some illnesses were so feared that anyone who had them was sent back to the ship immediately. But most illnesses could be treated. The sick were taken to dorms where they stayed until they were well again. Men stayed in one dorm, women in another. It was possible for an entire family to be turned away when one member was ill, especially if the person was a child.

Immigrants also took an intelligence test as they slowly moved up the stairs. This was not easy for some. The questions were in English, and not all immigrants spoke the language well. If they were over fourteen years of age, immigrants were asked to read a short text in their home language.

By the time they reached the top of the stairs, immigrants had passed the first tests.

In the Registry Room

Now immigrants faced legal tests to their entry into the United States. Translators helped them understand the questions. Inspectors asked, "Do you have a job waiting for you?" If the answer was "No," the immigrant might be turned away.

Immigrants often had letters from family already in the United States. They might have rail tickets to their new homes. These papers helped greatly. Most people passed the legal test in just a few minutes. They gladly gathered their belongings and took the ferry to New York City.

But some immigrants did not pass the legal test. They had to face more questions. Any woman traveling on her own had to have a family member or sponsor waiting for her. Otherwise, she was sent home. Sadly, now and then, a wife came with her children, only to find her husband could not come to claim her. When this happened, she had to take her children back to her home country.

The Ellis Island experience was scary for some immigrants. Coming to a new nation was risky. Still, most made it through the station in a day. During the 1920s, immigrants were required to pass all the tests before leaving their home port. This saved travelers from getting to America only to have to turn around and make a long and expensive trip back home.

Ellis Island closed in 1954. It is now a museum and a monument to the immigrants who chose to become Americans.

Name _____ Date _____

Now answer Numbers 14 through 18 on your Answer Sheet. Base your answers on the article "The Ellis Island Experience."

14 The author's description of the conditions in which most immigrants traveled best helps readers understand

    F. why passengers were checked so carefully for contagious illnesses.

    G. what immigrants were willing to tolerate in order to come to the United States.

    H. why immigrants wanted to leave their homelands behind to come to the United States.

    I. why many immigrants had to go through Ellis Island in order to enter the United States.

15 Read this sentence from the article.

> **Passengers who were ill had to be treated before being allowed to go ashore.**

Complete this analogy, based on how the word *ill* is used in the sentence above: *filthy* is to *clean* as *ill* is to

    A. happy.

    B. healthy.

    C. rough.

    D. unwell.

16 Which statement from the article presents the author's opinion on the processing of immigrants?

    F. "The Ellis Island experience was scary for some immigrants."

    G. "Other doctors checked each person for signs of contagious illness."

    H. "Most made it through the tests; about two percent had to return home."

    I. "Between 1892 and 1924, about twelve million immigrants entered the United States through Ellis Island."

Name _____ Date _____

17 In order to pass the legal test, a woman traveling alone had to

    A. already have a job waiting for her.

    B. possess a rail ticket to her new home.

    C. prove that she could speak English fluently.

    D. have a family member or sponsor waiting for her.

18 Which summary most accurately describes the use of Ellis Island?

    F. It served as a processing station for immigrants for more than six decades and is now a museum.

    G. It served as a processing station for immigrants for ten years and is now part of the New York skyline.

    H. It served as a processing station for immigrants for many years and continues to welcome immigrants today.

    I. It served as a processing station for immigrants for many years and is now the gateway to the Statue of Liberty.

Read the poem "Ode to an Otter" before answering Numbers 19 through 23.

Ode to an Otter

I ought to be an otter, 'cause when all is said and done
I could play along the riverbank, or stretch out in the sun.
I'd swim beneath the water, or backstroke up on top.
I'd dive in like a graceful swan, or do a belly flop.

My days would be so peaceful as a furry, swimming mammal
As opposed to bearing burdens like a one-humped desert camel.
I wouldn't want to herd sheep like a working collie dog
Or end up an amphibian—a turtle, toad, or frog.

But oh, to be an otter! It would be a stroke of luck
Just to spend all day a-swimmin', or a-rollin' in the muck.
But oh, as fate would have it, I'm required to spend my time
Doing schoolwork. What a pity. It seems like such a crime.

The month of May has ended, and all across the nation
The schools have shut their doors, and all of the kids are on vacation.
Yet here it's still the school year, and it can't end too soon,
But the days are standing still, stretching till the end of June.

Ah, the otter, who, when sunshine makes the heat rise at the shore,
Stays within its coolsome burrow, eating clams and snails and more.
It swims along the river, catching crayfish, frogs, and trout.
I'd be an awesome otter—of that I have no doubt.

Right now I watch the summer tapping at each window pane
And count the days till school is out, and I can swim again.
I'll walk in glorious mud that squeezes coolness through my toes
And skip along the river, free from tests and schoolwork woes.

Till then, I'll be an otter, but only in my head,
And start the summer early there, along the riverbed.
'Cause if I was an otter and could romp and roll and roam,
I wouldn't have to think of what to write for my class poem.

**Now answer Numbers 19 through 23 on your Answer Sheet. Base your answers
on the poem "Ode to an Otter."**

19 Read these lines from the poem.

> **My days would be so peaceful as a furry, swimming mammal / As
> opposed to bearing burdens like a one-humped desert camel.**

What does the word *burdens* mean in the sentence above?

A. doubts

B. feelings

C. objects

D. rivers

20 Read these lines from the poem.

> **Yet here it's still the school year, and it can't end too soon, / But the
> days are standing still, stretching till the end of June.**

What does the author mean by the phrase *the days are standing still*?

F. The days seem to pass by slowly.

G. The days are full of difficult work.

H. The speaker's school day is longer than at most schools.

I. There are more school days left than the speaker thought.

21 Read these lines from the poem.

> **I'll walk in glorious mud that squeezes coolness through my toes / And skip along the river, free from tests and schoolwork woes.**

How would the effect of these lines be different if the author had used the word *walk* instead of *skip*?

A. The speaker would seem less carefree.

B. The speaker would seem more friendly.

C. The speaker would seem to miss school.

D. The speaker would seem less serious.

22 What effect does the author's use of language such as *'cause, a-swimmin'*, and *awesome* create in the poem?

F. It makes the speaker sound casual.

G. It makes the speaker sound persuasive.

H. It makes the speaker seem caring toward all animals.

I. It makes the speaker seem knowledgeable about otters.

23 The end of the poem is ironic because the speaker

A. decides to write a poem about an otter.

B. turns into an otter and swims away from school.

C. changes her mind and doesn't want to be an otter.

D. has finished the poem that seemed too hard to write.

Read the passage "Five Boiled Eggs" before answering Numbers 24 through 29.

"I promise to pay you as soon as I can."

An Old Turkish Tale

Retold by Laura S. Sassi
illustrated by Allan Eitzen

Long ago, a poor country boy left home to seek his fortune. Day and night he traveled, stopping to eat at inns along the way. Though he ate sparingly, his money quickly dwindled until, one day, no silver *akches* remained.

Still, the boy kept walking. Soon, however, his empty belly began to ache. Staggering up to the next inn he saw, he approached the innkeeper.

"Please feed me!" he said. "I don't have any money now, but I promise to pay you as soon as I can."

"I'll see what I can spare," the innkeeper grumbled. He took five boiled eggs out of a large bowl and put them on a plate with some stale bread. "Here," he said, plopping the platter in front of the boy.

The famished lad gratefully gobbled every morsel. Then, repeating his promise to pay back the innkeeper, he journeyed on.

Revived by his five-egg breakfast, the boy soon reached a bustling seaport. Intent on finding his fortune, he set sail on the first ship that was leaving the harbor.

Years passed, and the lad prospered. As a sea merchant, he sailed far, stopping in many exotic ports. However, he never forgot his humble beginnings or the money he owed the innkeeper.

When he finally returned home, he stopped by the old roadside inn.

Name _____ Date _____

"Kind sir," he respectfully inquired, "how much for the five boiled eggs that you served me so long ago?"

In truth, the innkeeper did not remember him, for this fine-looking fellow looked nothing like the scrawny lad who had begged for food some ten years before. Still, eager to make a profit, he readily added up the charges. "That'll be ten thousand akches," he declared.

"For five eggs?" The rich stranger gasped. He had thought that he would have to pay no more than ten or twenty akches.

"Ah, but you must consider their lost worth," the greedy innkeeper replied. "Had you not eaten those eggs, they would have hatched into hens. Those hens, in turn, would have laid eggs that would have hatched into hens. . . ." On and on he ranted until at last he reached his grand total.

"Ah, but you must consider their lost worth."

When the stunned merchant refused to pay, the innkeeper declared that he would take him to court.

A trial was set for the following week. Alas, rumor had it that the judge was a close friend of the innkeeper.

"I'm ruined!" the merchant muttered as he sat in the village square. "What will I do?"

At that moment, he was approached by a sturdy little man wearing a white turban and riding a donkey. "Nasreddin Hodja, at your service," the man said with a friendly nod. "What seems to be the problem?"

After hearing the merchant's story, Hodja announced, "This is your lucky day! It would be my honor to defend you. I have great experience in these matters."

"Thank you," the merchant said, amazed at his good fortune.

"What seems to be the problem?"

But when the court date finally arrived, Nasreddin Hodja was nowhere in sight.

"Woe is me," mumbled the merchant.

"I'll soon be rich!" cried the innkeeper.

"Where is Hodja?" demanded the judge, growing angrier by the minute. He was about to render judgment in the innkeeper's favor when Hodja boldly barged in.

"Pardon me," he said, panting, as he hastily took the witness stand. "I would have been here sooner, but this morning I had the cleverest plan. Instead of eating my boiled corn for breakfast, I planted it. Think of the rich harvest I'll reap!"

"That's absurd," the innkeeper scoffed. "You can't grow corn from cooked kernels!"

"Indeed?" Hodja said with mock wonder. "Then, sir, how is it that you would have been able to hatch chickens from boiled eggs?"

At that, the whole room reeled with laughter.

"Order in the court!" shouted the judge, pounding his gavel and scowling at the innkeeper.

The judge then ruled that the merchant would not have to pay even one akche for the eggs. Instead, the innkeeper would have to pay a fine for wasting the court's time with such foolishness.

Now answer Numbers 24 through 29 on your Answer Sheet. Base your answers on the passage "Five Boiled Eggs."

24 Read this sentence from the passage.

> **Though he ate sparingly, his money quickly dwindled until, one day, no silver *akches* remained.**

What does the word *dwindled* mean in the sentence above?

   F. was spent wisely

   G. lost worth over time

   H. became gradually less

   I. was placed into savings

Name _____   Date _____

25 Read this excerpt from the passage.

> **Years passed, and the lad prospered. As a sea merchant, he sailed far, stopping in many exotic ports. However, he never forgot his humble beginnings or the money he owed the innkeeper.**

The excerpt above reveals that, unlike the innkeeper, the merchant is

A. honest.

B. arrogant.

C. content with his life.

D. ashamed of his background.

26 The people in the courtroom burst into laughter when they suddenly realize how

F. smart the merchant is.

G. ridiculous Hodja can be.

H. silly the innkeeper's claim is.

I. inexpensive boiled eggs really are.

27 In this passage, Nasreddin Hodja is shown to have both cleverness and

A. great fame.

B. great wealth.

C. a sense of humor.

D. a lack of common sense.

28 Because he took the merchant to court, the innkeeper must

F. pay a fine.

G. pay for the eggs.

H. buy dinner for Hodja.

I. apologize to the merchant.

29 Which of the following best describes a theme of this passage?

A. Humor can often get you out of a sticky situation.

B. Trying to pay someone back usually turns out bad.

C. Sometimes it is better to be lucky than to be clever.

D. It is unwise to take advantage of another person's kindness.

Read the article "The Newest Board Sport" before answering Numbers 30 through 35.

The Newest Board Sport

People spot them in airports or checking into a hotel—an excited group of city teenagers, known as the Raging Rooks. Sometimes, they carry a large, shiny trophy. People stare. A few ask, "What sport do you play?" or "Are you a singing group?" The answer is almost always a surprise.

These Harlem middle school boys are a chess team. Yes, ladies and gentlemen, *chess*. And they are champions. The Raging Rooks come from the Adam Clayton Powell Jr. Junior High School 43. Once, they tied for first place in the National Junior High Chess Championship, and along the way, they topped sixty other teams.

The Rooks are named for a chess piece called a rook, or castle. These young people are changing the common image of chess players: shy, dull, and, well, sort of . . . not cool. This hip team of teens challenges what people often think about chess: that kids will be bored by a board game.

How did these ordinary kids get the chance to become such winners? They learned in school. Since 1986, New York City's "Chess-in-the Schools" program has involved thousands of students. This program brings great chess players into the public schools. It brought the Raging Rooks their coach, Maurice Ashley.

One Cool Coach

Maurice Ashley, at the age of 33, became the world's first African American to earn the title of International Grandmaster. Grandmaster . . . sounds like a DJ or a karate instructor. Actually, it's the highest level of achievement in chess.

Born in Jamaica, Maurice Ashley grew up in Brooklyn, New York. He got serious about chess when he was 14. As he was first beginning to play, a friend beat him in a game . . . badly. Maurice Ashley's response was to hit the library, where he began to study chess books. He decided to play in local tournaments. He also improved his skills by playing members of the Black Bear School of Chess. This local group of African American masters helped feed his hunger for the game. The Black Bears held Friday night "chess rumbles." Here, he says, members attacked the game like fighters.

Maurice Ashley is known for his modern playing style, which is aggressive and determined. He has also been a guest announcer for famous chess meets. At the mike, he spices things up. He has also made the video "Maurice Ashley Teaches Chess," in which he uses sports comparisons to make the game more exciting.

Are Chess Players *Athletes*?

Maurice Ashley has worked to show that chess is a true sport—and a fun, cool one. He knows that people laugh when chess is compared to athletics. Let's face it, a chess move is nothing like shooting a three-pointer or leaping up a wall to catch a sure home run. However, what chess and all sports are about, he says, is not just what

Name _____ Date _____

fans see, but also the energy that goes *into* the game.

Top players like Maurice Ashley train hard in order to have the staying power for tournament play. One game can last as long as six hours; during this time, players need to remain focused. Their brains must be sharp and ready. "If I am not fit," Maurice Ashley explains in an interview for a Jamaican sports newsletter, "come round seven or eight . . . my tongue is hanging on the floor."

The Benefits of Playing Chess

- Chess improves memory and concentration.

- Chess encourages independent thinking as players make on-the-spot decisions.

- Chess develops players' ability to make predictions and to see ahead to what might happen next.

- Chess improves thinking in science and mathematics.

- Chess develops creativity and helps players use their imaginations.

- Chess helps players control their nerves and helps them learn patience.

- Chess gives players the chance to play, meet people, and have fun!

Now answer Numbers 30 through 35 on your Answer Sheet. Base your answers on the article "The Newest Board Sport."

30 Why would the Jamaican sports newsletter in which Maurice Ashley is quoted be considered a primary source?

    F. It was published relatively recently.

    G. It includes a direct interview with Ashley.

    H. It was produced after Maurice Ashley became a chess champion.

    I. It reviews important chess tournaments in which Ashley took part.

31 Read this excerpt from the article.

> **These Harlem middle school boys are a chess team. Yes, ladies and gentlemen, *chess*.**

The author's word choice in the excerpt helps create a tone that is

    A. conversational.

    B. dreamy.

    C. proud.

    D. serious.

32 Which detail from the article is an opinion about the Raging Rooks?

    F. The team's members are hip and exciting.

    G. The team has beaten at least 60 other teams.

    H. The team's members learned chess at school.

    I. The team comes from a junior high school in Harlem.

33 Read this excerpt from the article.

> **As he was first beginning to play, a friend beat him in a game . . .**
> **badly. Maurice Ashley's response was to hit the library, where he**
> **began to study chess books.**

What does the excerpt above reveal about Maurice Ashley?

A. He is loyal.

B. He is dedicated.

C. He plays chess for fun.

D. He didn't like chess at first.

34 Based on the way the author describes the game of chess, the Raging Rooks, and their coach, Maurice Ashley, readers can conclude that the author

F. is a serious and passionate chess player.

G. has little to no experience playing chess.

H. believes that chess is like any other sport.

I. respects the game of chess and its players.

35 Read this sentence from the article.

> **One game can last as long as six hours; during this time, players need**
> **to remain focused.**

Complete this analogy, based on how the word *focused* is used in the sentence above: *careful* is to *thorough* as *focused* is to

A. alert

B. sensible

C. sly

D. talented

Revising and Editing

Read the introduction and the passage "A Strange Event" before answering Numbers 1 through 7.

Andrew has written a passage about a strange event that happened. Read his passage and think about the changes he should make.

A Strange Event

(1) One early summer day in 1908, an unusual event took place near Vanavara, Russia. (2) However, the day began in its usual way with people going to work and to the market. (3) A man named Yakov boarded the train for the short trip to his workplace near Lake Baikal. (4) My mother's workplace is near a lake, too. (5) As he looked out the window, he suddenly saw a white fireball move very, really fast across the sky. (6) He stared at it in amazement. (7) Then, the object exploded. (8) It caused a flash so bright that Yakov had to cover his eyes. (9) The explosion sounded like thunder.

(10) The train shook from the force of the blast. (11) Passengers screamed. (12) They was crying and wringing their hands. (13) "Whoa what happened?" some asked in confusion. (14) "Look," shouted Yakov, "a huge black cloud is rising into the sky!"

Name _____ Date _____

(15) At home a couple of days later, Yakov sat with his family, reading

allowed from the newspaper. (16) "Homes as far as 650 kilometers away to

the blast had their windows broken," Yakov read. (17) "The air is hazy all the

way from Russia to London, England." (18) Yakov's children listened as he

continued to read. (19) "In one area 50 kilometers across, about 60 million

trees have been flattened." (20) Yakov shook his head in wonder. (21) They

were lucky to be alive!

(22) For years, scientists were not sure what had caused the strange event.

(23) Today, they believe it was a comet or a meteor exploding with the air.

(24) Whatever it was, Yakov and his fellow passengers never forgetted what

they saw that day.

Now answer Numbers 1 through 7 on your Answer Sheet. Base your answers on the changes Andrew should make.

1 What change should be made in sentence 5?

    A. change *looked* to **looks**

    B. delete the comma after *window*

    C. change *suddenly* to **sudden**

    D. change *move very, really fast* to **zoom**

2 What change should be made in sentence 12?

    F. change *They* to **They're**

    G. change *was* to **were**

    H. change *wringing* to **ringing**

    I. change *their* to **there**

Name _____ Date _____

3 What change should be made in sentence 13?

    A. delete the quotation marks before *Whoa*

    B. insert a comma after *Whoa*

    C. change *asked* to **asks**

    D. change the period to an exclamation point

4 What change should be made in sentence 15?

    F. change *couple* to **couples**

    G. delete the comma after *later*

    H. change *sat* to **set**

    I. change *allowed* to **aloud**

5 What change should be made in sentence 16?

    A. change *to* to **from**

    B. change *have* to **has**

    C. delete the comma after *broken*

    D. change *read* to **reads**

6 What change should be made in sentence 24?

    F. change *was* to **were**

    G. change *passengers* to **passengors**

    H. change *forgetted* to **forgot**

    I. change *saw* to **seen**

7 Which sentence does NOT belong in this passage?

    A. sentence 4

    B. sentence 8

    C. sentence 19

    D. sentence 22

Name _____ Date _____

Read the introduction and the passage "Tamisha's Idea" before answering Numbers 8 through 13.

Carla wrote this passage about a girl who visits the beach. Read her passage and think about the changes she should make.

Tamisha's Idea

(1) Tamisha was spending part of her vacation with her grandmother, who lived in a house on the coast. (2) Her house had a comfortable porch that faced the Atlantic Ocean. (3) You could step out the back door and be swimming in the ocean within a minute.

(4) Tamisha loved spending time with her grandmother. (5) She also enjoyed being next to the ocean. (6) However, this vacation wasn't going to be nonstop fun. (7) Before Tamisha returned home, she had to write and illustrate a children's book for art class. (8) Tamisha's art teacher was Ms. Hillerman. (9) Tamisha had brainstormed a list of ideas she still could not think of a topic for her book.

(10) As she was sitting on the porch with her grandmother one afternoon, Tamisha noticed the air was getting more humider. (11) She and her grandmother watched as the clouds over the ocean became thicker and darker. (12) They could tell it would begin to rain soon. (13) They went inside the house to observe the storm.

(14) After the rain had stopped, Tamisha went outside to splash in the puddles. (15) She knew it would not be long before the warm sun caused them to dry up. (16) Later, she went for a walk on the beach with her grandmother. (17) The seashells and driftwood that had been washed ashore by the storm

would make nice decorasions. (18) Tamisha picked up some and careful put them into a bucket she was carrying.

(19) As she collected a particularly beautiful shell, Tamisha had a very, really good idea. (20) Her children's book would be about the life and beauty of the seashore. (21) She would call her book *The Beautiful Beach.*

Now answer Numbers 8 through 13 on your Answer Sheet. Base your answers on the changes Carla should make.

8 What is the best way to revise sentence 9?

   F. Tamisha had brainstormed a list of ideas, but she still could not think of a topic for her book.

   G. Tamisha had brainstormed a list of ideas so she still could not think of a topic for her book.

   H. Tamisha had brainstormed a list of ideas, or she still could not think of a topic for her book.

   I. Tamisha had brainstormed a list of ideas however she still could not think of a topic for her book.

9 What change should be made in sentence 10?

   A. change *was* to **had**

   B. change *with* to **to**

   C. change *noticed* to **notices**

   D. change *more humider* to **more humid**

10 What change should be made in sentence 17?

   F. change *and* to **a comma**

   G. change *washed* to **wash**

   H. insert a comma after *ashore*

   I. change *decorasions* to **decorations**

Name _____ Date _____

11 What change should be made in sentence 18?

    A. change *up* to **on**

    B. change *careful* to **carefully**

    C. change *put* to **putted**

    D. change *carrying* to **carried**

12 What change should be made in sentence 19?

    F. change *beautiful* to **beautifully**

    G. insert a period after *shell*

    H. change *had* to **has**

    I. change *very, really good* to **wonderful**

13 Which sentence does NOT belong in this passage?

    A. sentence 6

    B. sentence 8

    C. sentence 11

    D. sentence 16

Read the introduction and the passage "Hearing Helper" before answering Numbers 14 through 19.

Jason has written a passage about a special dog. Read his passage and think about the changes he should make.

Hearing Helper

(1) Mini was an adorable terrier mix who has been living in the local animal shelter for a couple of years. (2) One day, Mr. Johnson came at the shelter to meet Mini and see if she would make a good hearing dog. (3) Mr. Johnson worked at a special center that trains service dogs.

(4) After meeting Mini and performing a few tests, Mr. Johnson knew she was the perfectly candidate to help a person who is hearing impaired. (5) He smiled and said, "I'd like to take her to our school so we can train her to be a service dog."

(6) Mini left the shelter with Mr. Johnson, and she started school right away. (7) She was an eager learner. (8) Mini could soon let her trainer know when she heard noises, such as a smoke alarm, an alarm clock, a telephone ringing, a doorbell, or a knock at the door. (9) Mini finally completed her training and she was ready to work with a person who had difficulty hearing or could not hear at all.

(10) Mini was scheduled to live with 12-year-old Lesa Anderson. (11) As soon Lesa saw Mini, Lesa knew they would be great friends. (12) Lesa and her parents spent a week at the school learning how to work with Mini. (13) Lesa was very excited about taking her new helper home.

(14) When the family arrived back at their home, Lesa showed Mini where her bedroom was. (15) She gave the dog a comfortable bed right next

Name _____ Date _____

to hers. (16) She gave Mini some toys to play with, too. (17) When Lesa went

to bed that night, she set her alarm clock. (18) When the alarm rang the next

morning, Mini woke up Lisa. (19) Mini woke up Lesa to begin their day

together.

_____

Now answer Numbers 14 through 19 on your Answer Sheet. Base your answers on the changes Jason should make.

14 What change should be made in sentence 1?

    F. change *who* to **which**

    G. change *has* to **had**

    H. change *local* to **locale**

    I. change *years* to **year's**

15 What change should be made in sentence 2?

    A. delete the comma after *day*

    B. change *came* to **comed**

    C. change *at* to **to**

    D. change *make* to **making**

16 What change should be made in sentence 4?

    F. insert a comma after *Mini*

    G. change *performing* to **perferming**

    H. change *knew* to **knowed**

    I. change *perfectly* to **perfect**

Name _____ Date _____

17 What change should be made in sentence 9?

A. change *finally* to **final**

B. change *her* to **hers**

C. insert a comma after *training*

D. change *could not* to **could'nt**

18 Which sentence could best follow sentence 11?

F. Lesa and her family used to have a cat and a goldfish.

G. Lesa fell in love with Mini's fuzzy face and playful personality.

H. Mini also learned how to lead her trainer to the sounds she heard.

I. The trainer spent several months teaching Mini how to be a hearing dog.

19 What is the best way to revise sentences 18 and 19?

A. When the alarm rang the next morning, Mini woke up Lesa to begin their day together.

B. When the alarm rang, the next morning, Mini woke up, Lesa to begin their day together.

C. When the alarm rang the next morning, but Mini woke up Lesa to begin their day together.

D. When the alarm rang the next morning, Mini and Lesa they begin their day together and woke up.

Read the introduction and the passage "A Dolphin" before answering Numbers 20 through 25.

Maria wrote this passage about a boy who sees a dolphin for the first time. Read her passage and think about the changes she should make.

A Dolphin

(1) "Dolphins are very super cool creatures," Tom told his little sister, Christina. (2) "I'd love to see one."

(3) The children stood next to their parents on the beach. (4) They looked out at the Atlantic Ocean, which seemed to stretch on forever. (5) The sun felt warm on their faces.

(6) Gentle waves splashed on the beach, making the sand feel squishy under their toes. (7) First, Christina giggled and bent down to touch the sand with her fingers. (8) After, Dad held her and helped her swim in the shallow water. (9) Meanwhile, Tom pretended to be a dolphin, he popped up and down in the water. (10) He swam in circles around his parents.

(11) Tom stopped swimming for a few moments. (12) "Did you know that dolphins are mammals?" Tom asked. (13) "They can swim underwater." (14) "They have to come up for air just like me." (15) Tom knew a lot about dolphins because he had a book about them at home.

(16) Just then anything in the ocean caught Tom's eye. (17) He could see a small fishing boat. (18) He could see a shape moving quickly in front of it. (19) Then it hit him. (20) He was seeing a bottlenose dolphin for the first time in his life!

(21) He pointed the dolphin out to his family, and they all watched it swim around the boat and they wished it would jump. (22) They were fascinated by

Name _____ Date _____

how playful the dolphin seemed. (23) Before long, the dolphin jumped high
into the air and then disappeared back into the ocean. (24) Tom could not wait
to tell his friends about what he had seen.

Now answer Numbers 20 through 25 on your Answer Sheet. Base your answers on the changes Maria should make.

20 What changes should be made in sentence 1?

    F. change *Dolphins* to **Dolphin's**

    G. change *very super cool* to **amazing**

    H. change *creatures* to **creaters**

    I. delete the quotation marks

21 What change should be made in sentence 8?

    A. change *After* to **Then**

    B. change *Dad* to **dad**

    C. change *in* to **with**

    D. change *shallow* to **not too deeply**

22 What change should be made in sentence 9?

    F. change *Meanwhile* to **So**

    G. change *pretended* to **pretending**

    H. insert **and** after *dolphin,*

    I. insert a comma after *up*

23 What is the best way to combine sentences 13 and 14?

    A. "They can swim underwater, come up for air, just like me."

    B. "They can swim underwater, have to come up for air just like me."

    C. "They can swim underwater, but they have to come up for air just like me."

    D. "They can swim underwater so have to come up for air just like me they do."

24 What change should be made in sentence 16?

    F. change *anything* to **something**

    G. insert a comma after *ocean*

    H. change *caught* to **catched**

    I. change *Tom's* to **Toms**

25 What is the best way to revise sentences 17 and 18?

    A. He could see a small fishing boat and a shape moving quickly in front of it.

    B. He could see a small fishing boat in front of it a small shape moving quickly.

    C. He could see, a small fishing boat, and a shape, moving quickly in front of it.

    D. He could see a small fishing boat, and could see a shape moving quickly in front of it.

Name _____ Date _____

Writing Opinions

Read the passage "Thelma B. Still: A Tall Tale" before responding to the prompt.

Thelma B. Still
A Tall Tale

Thelma B. Still was the loudest woman on the East Coast. Her voice was so loud that you could hear it from as far away as California. When she woke up each day and said "Good morning," the sky filled with thousands of birds trying to fly away from what they thought was a terrible thunderstorm.

Everyone liked Thelma. They all knew she didn't mean any harm, but they couldn't talk to her without their ears hurting. Folks had to talk to her while standing about 500 feet away from her so their eardrums wouldn't explode.

Sometimes, though, Thelma's loudness was helpful. Parents needed her help if their children didn't come when called in for supper. All it took was one bellow from Thelma—a long, drawn-out "John!" or "Anne!" or "Matthew!" There would soon be an answering call of "Coming, Mom!" or "Coming, Dad!"

Unfortunately, there were more than a few Johns, Annes, and Matthews in the county. It often got pretty confusing with all those kids showing up at their front doors looking for supper.

Things might have gone on like this for some time if it hadn't been for Pearl Macpherson's troublesome cat. Her cat solved the biggest noise problem east of the Mississippi River. Here is how it happened.

The cat's name was Whiskers. It was not a very original name for a cat, but it was the only name to which he would answer. He had been missing for a week. Pearl called and called his name, but there was no answer and no cat. If he didn't answer soon, she was going to get another cat.

Finally, someone suggested having Thelma call for the cat since he was sure to hear her, wherever he was. So Pearl went to Thelma's house to ask for her help. Thelma agreed. After Pearl was a safe distance away, Thelma stepped off her front porch and said "Whiskers!" three times.

The two women heard something high up in the trees. It sounded like a scream in pain, but it was definitely a cat making the sound. Whiskers was stuck at the top of a tree and had most likely been chased up there by a wild animal.

"Oh," said Pearl, "I forgot to tell you that Whiskers is afraid of loud noises. You've probably scared him even more than he was before."

Thelma, who loved animals, was upset by Pearl's remark. She ran into the house to find something to wipe away her tears. The only thing she could find was a thick scarf that her mother had made for her. She came out holding the scarf to her face and muttering, "Oh, Whiskers, I didn't mean to scare you!"

It was amazing. Thelma wasn't loud anymore. Why, you could hardly hear her with the scarf held up to her face. Whiskers came right down from that tree.

Since then, whenever Thelma talks to someone, she holds the scarf to her face. That's why we call that scarf a "muffler." When Thelma has to call the kids or the cows or the cats to come home, she drops the muffler and just hollers. In fact, if you listen really hard around noon each day, you'll hear her announcing lunchtime. She's been announcing lunch at the wool factory ever since their noon whistle broke.

Now respond to the prompt. Base your response on the passage "Thelma B. Still: A Tall Tale."

> Movies are sometimes based on existing literature.
>
> Think about whether or not this passage would make a good movie.
>
> Now write a response that tells why you think this passage would or would not make a good movie.

Planning Page

Use this space to make your notes before you begin writing. The writing on this page will NOT be scored.

_____

_____

_____

_____

_____

_____

_____

_____

_____

_____

_____

_____

_____

_____

_____

_____

Name _____ Date _____

Begin writing your response here. The writing on this page and the next page WILL be scored.

_____

_____

_____

_____

_____

_____

_____

_____

_____

_____

_____

_____

_____

_____

_____

_____

_____

_____

_____

_____

_____

_____

_____

_____

_____

Name _____   Date _____

_____

_____

_____

_____

_____

_____

_____

_____

_____

_____

_____

_____

_____

_____

_____

_____

_____

_____

_____

_____

_____

_____

_____

_____

_____

_____

Reading Complex Text

Read the passage "School Days of an Indian Girl: The Cutting of My Long Hair" and the poem "I Am a Part of the Dragon." As you read, stop and answer each question. Use evidence from the passage and the poem to support your answers.

School Days of an Indian Girl: The Cutting of My Long Hair

from *American Indian Stories* by Zitkala-Sa

Zitkala-Sa, or Gertrude Bonnin, was born in 1876. She grew up on a Sioux reservation in South Dakota. At age eight, as part of a U.S. government policy designed to "Americanize" American Indian children, she was sent east to a boarding school.

The first day in the land of apples was a bitter-cold one; for the snow still covered the ground, and the trees were bare. A large bell rang for breakfast, its loud metallic voice crashing through the belfry overhead and into our sensitive ears. The annoying clatter of shoes on bare floors gave us no peace. The constant clash of harsh noises, with an undercurrent of many voices murmuring an unknown tongue, made a bedlam within which I was securely tied. And though my spirit tore itself in struggling for its lost freedom, all was useless.

A paleface woman, with white hair, came up after us. We were placed in a line of girls who were marching into the dining room. These were Indian girls, in stiff shoes and closely clinging dresses. The small girls wore sleeved aprons and shingled hair. As I walked noiselessly in my soft moccasins, I felt like sinking to the floor, for my blanket had been stripped from my shoulders. While we marched in, the boys entered at an opposite door. I watched for the three young braves who came in our party. I spied them in the rear ranks, looking as uncomfortable as I felt. A small bell was tapped, and each of the pupils drew a chair from under the table. Supposing this act meant they were to be seated, I pulled out mine and at once slipped into it from one side. But when I turned my head, I saw that I was the only one seated, and all the rest at our table remained standing. Just as I began to rise, looking shyly around to see how chairs were to be used, a second bell was sounded. All were seated at last, and I had to crawl back into my chair again. I heard a man's voice at one end of the hall, and I looked around to see him. But all the others hung their heads over their plates. As I glanced at the long chain of tables, I caught the eyes of a paleface woman upon me. Immediately I dropped my eyes, wondering why I was so keenly watched by the strange woman. The man ceased his mutterings, and then a third bell was tapped. Every one picked up his knife and fork and began eating. I began crying instead, for by this time I was afraid to venture anything more.

But this eating by formula was not the hardest trial in that first day. Late in the morning, my friend Judéwin gave me a terrible warning. Judéwin knew a few words of English; and she had overheard the paleface woman talk about cutting our long, heavy hair. Our mothers had taught us that only unskilled warriors who were captured had their hair shingled by the enemy. Among our people, short hair was worn by mourners, and shingled hair by cowards!

Name _____ Date _____

We discussed our fate some moments, and when Judéwin said, "We have to submit, because they are strong," I rebelled.

"No, I will not submit! I will struggle first!" I answered.

> ❶ How is Zitkala-Sa's response to having her hair cut different from Judéwin's response?
>
> _____
>
> _____
>
> _____

I watched my chance, and when no one noticed, I disappeared. I crept up the stairs as quietly as I could in my squeaking shoes—my moccasins had been exchanged for shoes. Along the hall I passed, without knowing whither I was going. Turning aside to an open door, I found a large room with three white beds in it. The windows were covered with dark green curtains, which made the room very dim. Thankful that no one was there, I directed my steps toward the corner farthest from the door. On my hands and knees I crawled under the bed, and cuddled myself in the dark corner.

From my hiding place I peered out, shuddering with fear whenever I heard footsteps nearby. Though in the hall loud voices were calling my name, and I knew that even Judéwin was searching for me, I did not open my mouth to answer. Then the steps were quickened and the voices became excited. The sounds came nearer and nearer. Women and girls entered the room. I held my breath and watched them open closet doors and peep behind large trunks. Someone threw up the curtains, and the room was filled with sudden light. What caused them to stoop and look under the bed I do not know. I remember being dragged out, though I resisted by kicking and scratching wildly. In spite of myself, I was carried downstairs and tied fast in a chair.

I cried aloud, shaking my head all the while until I felt the cold blades of the scissors against my neck, and heard them gnaw off one of my thick braids. Then I lost my spirit. Since the day I was taken from my mother I had suffered extreme indignities. People had stared at me. I had been tossed about in the air like a wooden puppet. And now my long hair was shingled like a coward's! In my anguish I moaned for my mother, but no one came to comfort me.

> ❷ From Zitkala-Sa's point of view, what did the cutting of her braids signify?
>
> _____
>
> _____
>
> _____

Name _____ Date _____

I Am a Part of the Dragon

I am a girl of the Great Dragon.

He is not a monster.

He is my brother, my uncle, my grandmother.

He is good luck, prosperity, and love.

Each Chinese New Year,

on the fifteenth day of the first month,

I put on my red and gold costume

and take my place

at the tail of the dragon.

I dance in perfect time

behind the great, scaled body

as it makes its way through

the lantern-lit streets of Chinatown.

While I am not yet strong enough

to work the gigantic head of the great creature,

I know that I am still important.

We must all work together to make him dance.

As his head dips low and lifts back up,

I must follow right behind.

As he sweeps his great head

from left to right, I too, follow,

sweeping my tail from left to right.

I can see my mother and my father beaming

from the sidewalk as we pass.

I am a part of this great ceremony

doing my part

to bring good things to my family this year.

I am a part of the dragon.

---

3 What overall effect does the arrangement of lines in the poem create?

_____

_____

_____

Name _____ Date _____

4 What is a similar theme between the passage and the poem? What evidence supports this?

_____

_____

_____

_____

_____

Reading and Analyzing Text

Read the passages "Ready . . . Set . . . Paddle!" and "Run, Run, Run!" before answering Numbers 1 through 18.

Ready . . . Set . . . Paddle!

Jamal Washington and his dad were going to participate in a river race on a stretch of the Colorado River that ran through Austin. Before this year, Jamal had been too young to take part in the race, even with an adult. He was glad he had turned eleven in time for the race. The race was held each year to get the public interested in the river's health and the importance of taking care of our waterways[1].

Mr. Washington loved to canoe, and he always liked the view of the gorgeous city skyline from the water. Jamal mainly wanted to have the fun of experiencing something new with his father. Neither particularly cared if they won or lost, but they were determined to try their best.

The race was timed, so it would be short but fast. The Washingtons had watched the race before, and they knew they would have to paddle steadily, working as a team. Jamal was in charge of making sure they had the required safety equipment. He had gathered helmets and life jackets for both of them. Mr. Washington believed in the advantages that good training offered, so he and Jamal had set a schedule and followed it.

The pair spent several weekends practicing paddling until they were confident that they worked efficiently. They simply moved as quickly as they could. It was important that they focus and not worry about how much time it would take them to complete the course.

On the day of the race, the paddling teams had to transport their boats to the launch site by 9:00 in the morning. The race would begin at 9:30 on the dot. The Washingtons arrived at the site at 8:00, and the shore was already crowded with other teams. Many of the teams were made up of parents and their children, and Jamal could not stop grinning. He was part of something big, exciting, and fun!

[1] **waterways:** bodies of water used for travel and transport

Name _____ Date _____

Run, Run, Run!

A marathon is a foot race that is just over 26 miles long. One such race is held in Austin, Texas, every year. People come from around the world to run in the Austin Marathon. Runners who complete this marathon fast enough can enter the Boston Marathon.

Shelly Anderson loved to run, and so did her older sister, Karen. Karen was graduating from high school this year, and she had registered for the race. She had trained for months, running up and down the hills in Austin. Karen knew she would have to adjust her pace to the hills and flat areas. She hoped to make it to the finish line, but she knew she might get too tired and have to drop out.

Shelly was excited to be able to watch her sister run. The media would televise the race, so Shelly knew her friends at home could watch Karen, too.

The racecourse would be open for seven hours. During the race, it would be lined with crowds of cheering supporters. Thousands of people registered for the event. Many runners ran to compete, and many others walked or ran just for the fun of it. The Anderson family promised to be there to cheer Karen on and take photographs of her during the race.

One theme of the race was "26 miles for 26 Charities." Nonprofit groups set up water stations along the race route so runners and walkers could get a drink. It was also a way for the charities to increase awareness of their work. Shelly looked forward to seeing the booths and hearing the bands that came out to play music and encourage the runners.

Shelly liked that her town had one of the "greenest" races in America. All plastic bottles were recycled. Refreshments were served on recyclable paper products. Solar energy was used to power lights on the stages for the bands.

All things considered, Shelly knew she would have a wonderful time cheering for Karen and watching the finalists cross the finish line.

Now answer Numbers 1 through 18 on your Answer Sheet. Base your answers on the passages "Ready . . . Set . . . Paddle!" and "Run, Run, Run!"

1 Read this sentence from the passage "Ready . . . Set . . . Paddle!"

> **Mr. Washington loved to canoe, and he always liked the view of the gorgeous city skyline from the water.**

What does the word *gorgeous* mean as used in the sentence above?

A. beautiful

B. cloudy

C. modern

D. mysterious

2 The reader can conclude from the passage "Ready . . . Set . . . Paddle!" that

F. children ages 10 and younger cannot be in the race.

G. only a certain number of people can participate in the race.

H. there must be two adults in every canoe or kayak in the race.

I. people who are watching the race must help clean up the river.

3 Read this sentence from the passage "Ready . . . Set . . . Paddle!"

> **Jamal was in charge of making sure they had the required safety equipment.**

What does the word *required* mean as used in the sentence above?

A. athletic

B. fashionable

C. necessary

D. ordinary

Name _____ Date _____

4 Read this sentence from the passage "Ready . . . Set . . . Paddle!"

> Mr. Washington believed in the advantages that good training offered,
> so he and Jamal had set a schedule and followed it.

What does the word *advantages* mean as used in the sentence above?

F. benefits

G. confidence

H. entertainment

I. lessons

5 Read the chart about the passage "Ready . . . Set . . . Paddle!"

Detail: Jamal and his dad are excited about participating in the river race.	Detail: Jamal is looking forward to doing something new with his dad.	Detail: Jamal and his dad work well together.
↓	↓	↓
Theme:		

Which sentence best completes the chart?

A. It is scary to try new things.

B. It is important to respect your family.

C. Learning new skills is often hard work.

D. Family members can have fun working together.

6 Read this sentence from the passage "Ready . . . Set . . . Paddle!"

> On the day of the race, the paddling teams had to transport their
> boats to the launch site by 9:00 in the morning.

Which word has the same Latin root as the word *transport* in the sentence above?

F. porcupine

G. portable

H. spoke

I. sport

7 Read this sentence from the passage "Ready . . . Set . . . Paddle!"

The race would begin at 9:30 on the dot.

What does the phrase *on the dot* mean in the sentence above?

  A. in the morning

  B. after the signal

  C. beside the shore

  D. at the exact time

8 The reader can conclude from the passage "Run, Run, Run!" that

  F. children of all ages can run in marathons.

  G. marathons are always held to support charities.

  H. the Boston Marathon takes place after the Austin Marathon.

  I. the Austin Marathon has more runners than any other marathon.

9 Read this sentence from the passage "Run, Run, Run!"

**The media would televise the race, so Shelly knew her friends at home
could watch Karen, too.**

What does the word *televise* mean as used in the sentence above?

  A. provide prize money for

  B. create advertising posters for

  C. broadcast pictures and sounds of

  D. publish newspaper articles about

10 Read this sentence from the passage "Run, Run, Run!"

> The Anderson family promised to be there to cheer Karen on and take photographs of her during the race.

Which part of the word *photographs* means "write"?

F. photo

G. pho

H. tog

I. graph

11 Read this sentence from the passage "Run, Run, Run!"

> Nonprofit groups set up water stations along the race route so runners and walkers could get a drink.

What does the word *stations* mean as used in the sentence above?

A. places to stop

B. police headquarters

C. buildings where trains stop

D. television or radio channels

12 Read this sentence from the passage "Run, Run, Run!"

> It was also a way for the charities to increase awareness of their work.

What does the word *awareness* mean as used in the sentence above?

F. dismay

G. enjoyment

H. knowledge

I. quality

Name _____ Date _____

13 Read this sentence from the passage "Run, Run, Run!"

Refreshments were served on recyclable paper products.

Which word has the same base word as the word *refreshments* in the
sentence above?

A. apartment

B. freshly

C. mental

D. refreeze

14 Read this sentence from the passage "Run, Run, Run!"

**All things considered, Shelly knew she would have a wonderful time
cheering for Karen and watching the finalists cross the finish line.**

Which word has the same suffix as the word *finalists* in the sentence above?

F. artist

G. insist

H. list

I. wrist

15 The reader can conclude from the passage "Run, Run, Run!" that Karen Anderson

A. taught her sister how to run.

B. is the best runner in her school.

C. hopes she will win the marathon.

D. believes it is important to practice.

16 Based on these two passages, what can the reader conclude about races in Austin, Texas?

    F. Few people prepare for them.

    G. They are all held on the water.

    H. Many people come to watch them.

    I. All participants have to wear helmets.

17 The reader can conclude from the passages that Jamal and Karen both

    A. would be successful at nearly any sport they tried.

    B. are more concerned with doing their best than with winning.

    C. would not participate in a race whose organizers did not care about the environment.

    D. will not enter any more races because of the amount of preparation they have to do.

18 Which of the following is an important idea in both passages?

    F. Life is full of interesting surprises.

    G. There is never enough time in the day.

    H. It can be fun to do something challenging.

    I. It is frustrating to try things that are too difficult.

Read the passage "Mayan Myths and Ruins" before answering Numbers 19 through 35.

Mayan Myths and Ruins

Last summer, the Salazar family went to visit the ancient Mayan ruins in Palenque (pah-LENG-keh), Mexico. The family took a trip to a historical site once every few years. Mom believed it was important for the children, Carlos and Juana, to learn about their Mexican heritage. She said, "We have a proud history with many stories that tell us how we became what we are today. Part of our history is best expressed in the architecture of the past. Our myths and legends reveal even more."

Therefore, the family's destination was one of the many "lost cities" of the Maya. Dad had gone to the local bookstore to get information on Palenque as well as new stories for the family to read. This time, he found a book of Mayan folktales.

On the Road to Palenque

The trip by car from their home in San Cristobal de las Casas, Mexico, would take about five hours. Carlos and Juana knew from experience that they would have plenty of time to entertain the family from the back seat of their car. Carlos and Juana had scanned the book of folktales their father brought home, each hoping to choose a tale that would be retold in the car. Their parents enjoyed the children's interpretations, and the storytelling was always a fun treat for the whole family.

Carlos chose the folktale of how the mockingbird became the best singer of all birds. Normally, Carlos and Juana would argue and try to persuade each other that their story was best, but Juana liked the story as much as Carlos. The children told the story of the mockingbird together. Everyone laughed when the two would interrupt each other in their excitement to tell the tale.

The Mockingbird's Tale

The mockingbird's family could not afford to dress in beautiful feathers. However, the little mockingbird had a beautiful singing voice. One day she took a job as a servant for a noble bird family. Meanwhile, this family of brilliantly colored cardinals had a young daughter. Her father wanted her to become a skilled singer, so he hired a famous singer to teach his daughter.

During the daughter's singing lessons, the young mockingbird hid and listened as the teacher tried to show the daughter how to sing. However, the only sound she could produce was a whistle. Soon the teacher realized his efforts with the daughter were

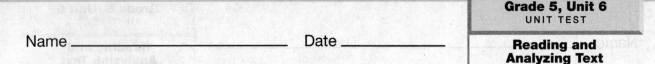
hopeless, and he left. The little mockingbird, however, had learned something from his lessons, and she practiced all day long.

One day, the cardinal decided that his daughter should give a concert for their friends. His daughter was scared, knowing she couldn't sing. Then she heard the mockingbird singing sweetly. The daughter begged the mockingbird to help her, and the mockingbird agreed.

The two asked a woodpecker to create a hole in a tree trunk where the mockingbird could hide during the concert. The daughter would pretend to sing, but the mockingbird would do the singing for her. They didn't think that the father cardinal would see the mockingbird crawl into the hole, but he did. However, he said nothing about it. He wanted to see what his daughter was doing.

The audience was impressed by the beautiful singing. It was the most beautiful singing they had ever heard! At the end of the concert, the father called for the mockingbird to come out of her hole. The plain mockingbird proved to be the real singer, and from then on, all mockingbirds inherited her beautiful voice. The cardinals, despite their beautiful color, never learned to sing.

Discovered Ruins

The children's parents cheered loudly at the end of the story. Then it was Mom's turn to teach everyone a little about Palenque. She described it as a ruined city tucked into a thick forest on a steep hill. From the tops of the ruined temples, sweeping views of the plains stretched to the ocean. It is an amazing sight.

Palenque was deserted sometime after the tenth century. The jungle took over and covered many of the buildings with plant life. Its location was unknown to Europeans until 1773. Since then, much has been learned about Palenque, and exciting new things are still being discovered today.

Almost There!

Mom suddenly stopped describing Palenque to her family. She wouldn't tell them anything else! She said the best way to learn about a place is through personal exploration and discovery. The family had heard enough to feel growing excitement at the prospect of seeing Palenque for themselves. Now they were almost there!

Name _____ Date _____

Now answer Numbers 19 through 35 on your Answer Sheet. Base your answers on the passage "Mayan Myths and Ruins."

19 The purpose of the illustration is to show

A. where Palenque is located.

B. when Palenque was deserted.

C. what some Mayan ruins look like.

D. how important folktales are in Mayan culture.

20 Read this sentence from the passage.

> Normally, Carlos and Juana would argue and try to persuade each other that their story was best, but Juana liked the story as much as Carlos.

What does the word *persuade* mean as used in the sentence above?

F. convince

G. fight

H. pretend

I. prevent

21 While traveling to Palenque, Carlos and Juana

A. play a game.

B. retell a folktale.

C. read silently.

D. invent a story.

22 Read this sentence from the passage.

> **Everyone laughed when the two would interrupt each other in their excitement to tell the tale.**

What does the word *interrupt* mean as used in the sentence above?

F. disagree with someone

G. entertain with a story

H. compare and contrast two things

I. speak while another person is talking

23 Read this sentence from the passage.

> **One day she took a job as a servant for a noble bird family.**

What does the word *noble* mean as used in the sentence above?

A. colorful

B. hardworking

C. high-ranking

D. quick-witted

24 Which of the following ideas from the selection is an opinion?

F. San Cristobal de las Casas is located in Mexico.

G. Jungle plants grew over the ruined city of Palenque.

H. The people who lived in Palenque left many centuries ago.

I. Exciting things are being discovered about Palenque today.

25 Read this sentence from the passage.

> **However, the only sound she could produce was a whistle.**

Which word has the same prefix as the word *produce* in the sentence above?

A. proceed

B. promptly

C. proven

D. prowling

Name _____   Date _____

26   Read this sentence from the passage.

> **Soon the teacher realized his efforts with the daughter were hopeless, and he left.**

What does the word *hopeless* mean as used in the sentence above?

F.   without hope

G.   before hoping

H.   one who hopes

I.   the act of hoping

27   Read this sentence from the passage.

> **One day, the cardinal decided that his daughter should give a concert for their friends.**

Which of the following shows the correct way to divide the word *concert* into syllables?

A.   con • cert

B.   co • ncert

C.   co • nc • ert

D.   conc • ert

28   Read this sentence from the passage.

> **The two asked a woodpecker to create a hole in a tree trunk where the mockingbird could hide during the concert.**

What does the word *trunk* mean as used in the sentence above?

F.   a tree's stem

G.   a part of a car

H.   a hard suitcase

I.   an elephant's nose

Name _____ Date _____

29 The cardinals in the selection are

    A. bossy and unkind.

    B. spoiled and silly.

    C. pretty but not able to sing.

    D. friendly but not willing to share.

30 Read this sentence from the passage.

    The audience was impressed by the beautiful singing.

In the above sentence, the word *audience* means people who

    F. organize a concert.

    G. listen to a performance.

    H. sing songs for others.

    I. choose an entertainer.

31 Which of the following ideas from the selection is an opinion?

    A. There are ruined temples in Palenque.

    B. The views from Palenque are amazing.

    C. Much has been learned about Palenque since 1773.

    D. Palenque is a ruined city in a thick forest on a steep hill.

32 Read this sentence from the passage.

    **From the tops of the ruined temples, sweeping views of the plains
stretched to the ocean. It is an amazing sight.**

What does the word *sweeping* mean in the sentence above?

    F. wild and dangerous

    G. bustling with activity

    H. taking in a wide area

    I. full of interesting details

Name _____ Date _____

33 "Mayan Myths and Ruins" is mostly about

    A. a mockingbird that helps a cardinal by singing for her in a concert.

    B. a family that learns about Mayan culture and travels to see Mayan ruins.

    C. two children who compete to see which one can tell the best story for their parents.

    D. a mother who wants her children to read stories about the ruined city of Palenque.

34 To find out when Palenque was discovered by Europeans, the reader should look at the text under the heading

    F. On the Road to Palenque.

    G. The Mockingbird's Tale.

    H. Discovered Ruins.

    I. Almost There!

35 Read this sentence from the passage.

> **The family had heard enough to feel growing excitement at the prospect of seeing Palenque for themselves.**

Which word has the same Latin root as the word *prospect* in the sentence above?

    A. property

    B. protection

    C. specialty

    D. spectator

Name _____ Date _____

Revising and Editing

Read the introduction and the article "Metric Measurements" before answering Numbers 1 through 7.

Donovan wrote an article about metric measurements. Read his article and think about the changes he should make.

Metric Measurements

(1) You may know that 1 foot is about as long as a book you use in school. (2) Your desk weighs several pounds. (3) Feet and pounds are kinds of measurements that most people in the United States use. (4) However, people in other countries use the metric system. (5) It has different units for measurement. (6) Meters, kilometers, centimeters and millimeters are used for length. (7) Grams and kilograms are used for weight.

(8) A meter is the metric systems' standard unit of length. (9) Look at a doorknob. (10) The distence from the doorknob to the floor is about 1 meter. (11) You can easily see thats a little longer than 1 yard, or 3 feet. (12) This can help you understand other metric amounts of length. (13) One kilometer is much longer than 1 meter—1,000 times longer, to be exact. (14) One centimeter is much smaller than 1 meter. (15) It takes 100 centimeters to make 1 meter. (16) One millimeter is even smaller. (17) In fact it takes 10 millimeters to make 1 centimeter.

(18) Plus, there is a standard unit of weight in the metric system. (19) It is called a gram. (20) A paper clip, a dime, and a raisin all weigh about 1 gram. (21) A person would weigh a lot of grams, so kilograms are used to weigh people and other large things. (22) There are 1,000 grams in 1 kilogram. (23) One kilogram is equal to about 2.2 pounds.

Name _____ Date _____

(24) The US government has decided not to change to the metric system

yet, but it is often used in science, even in our country.

_____

Now answer Numbers 1 through 7 on your Answer Sheet. Base your answers on the changes Donovan should make.

1 What change should be made in sentence 6?

   A. change *kilometers* to **Kilometers**

   B. insert a comma after *centimeters*

   C. change *used* to **uses**

   D. change *length* to **lenth**

2 What change should be made in sentence 8?

   F. change *the* to **a**

   G. change *systems'* to **system's**

   H. change *unit* to **Unit**

   I. change *of* to **in**

3 What change should be made in sentence 10?

   A. change *distence* to **distance**

   B. insert a comma after *doorknob*

   C. change *to* to **on**

   D. change *is* to **are**

4 What change should be made in sentence 11?

   F. insert **most** after *can*

   G. change *easily* to **easy**

   H. change *thats* to **that's**

   I. change *feet* to **foots**

5 What change should be made in sentence 17?

    A. insert a comma after *In fact*

    B. change *takes* to **took**

    C. change *centimeter* to **centimeters**

    D. change the period to a question mark

6 What change should be made in sentence 18?

    F. change *Plus* to **In addition**

    G. change *there* to **they're**

    H. change *weight* to **wait**

    I. change *in* to **from**

7 What change should be made in sentence 24?

    A. change *The* to **A**

    B. change *US* to **U.S.**

    C. delete the comma after *yet*

    D. change *our* to **ours**

Read the introduction and the article "Space Elevators" before answering Numbers 8 through 13.

Makayla wrote this article about space elevators. Read her article and think about the changes she should make.

Space Elevators

(1) Have you ever ridden in an elevator to the top floor of a building?

(2) Now, imagine if the elevator kept going up, all the way into outer space.

(3) For a long time people have dreamed of that possibility. (4) Mr Arthur C. Clarke, a well-known science fiction writer, was one of those people. (5) In the late 1970s, he wrote a book about an elevator that could stretch into space.

(6) Today, scientists are considering how to make Clarkes idea come true.

(7) A space elevator would need to be created from extremely strong materials. (8) Scientists are hoping to develop a new material that is strong, bendable, and durable. (9) Durable means long-lasting. (10) This product would be fashioned into a ribbon, and the ribbon would wind around a center piece. (11) This would be similar to the way thread is spun around a spool.

(12) The spool of ribbon would travel into space onboard a spacecraft.

(13) The spacecraft would circle Earth while the bottom end of the ribbon would flow down to Earth. (14) Next the ribbon would attach to a base on

Name _____ Date _____

the ocean floor. (15) The top end of the ribbon would remain in space and be

attached to a space object, such as a space station, an asteroid or a satellite.

(16) The ribbon would operate like a track. (17) A special vehicle would

run up and down the track. (18) It would use electricity made by the sun to

operate. (19) The elevator could be used every day, and its schedule would

not be disrubted by bad weather. (20) A space elevator could be useful.

(21) Perhaps we'll all get to ride it someday!

Now answer Numbers 8 through 13 on your Answer Sheet. Base your answers on the changes Makayla should make.

8 What change should be made in sentence 4?

    F. insert a period after **Mr**

    G. delete the period after *C*

    H. change *science* to **sience**

    I. delete the comma after **writer**

9 What change should be made in sentence 6?

    A. delete the comma after **Today**

    B. change *are* to **is**

    C. insert a colon after *considering*

    D. change *Clarkes* to **Clarke's**

10 What is the best way to revise sentences 8 and 9?

   F. Scientists are hoping to develop a new material that is strong, bendable, durable, and is long-lasting.

   G. Scientists are hoping to develop a new material that is strong, bendable, and durable (long-lasting).

   H. Scientists are hoping to develop a new material that is strong, bendable, and durable: long-lasting.

   I. Scientists are hoping to develop a new material that is strong, bendable, and durable, and it means long-lasting.

11 What change should be made in sentence 14?

   A. insert a comma after **Next**

   B. change *would* to **does**

   C. change *to* to **from**

   D. change *base* to **bace**

12 What change should be made in sentence 15?

   F. change *would* to **wood**

   G. change *remain* to **remained**

   H. insert a colon after **object**

   I. insert a comma after **asteroid**

13 What change should be made in sentence 19?

   A. change *its* to **it's**

   B. change *disrubted* to **disrupted**

   C. change *by* to **buy**

   D. change *weather* to **whether**

Read the introduction and the article "Interactive Art" before answering Numbers 14 through 19.

Laura wrote an article about interactive art for the school newspaper. Read her article and think about the changes she should make.

Interactive Art

(1) If you know how to use a computer you can create your own artistic vision. (2) It is called interactive art. (3) In interactive art, a person and the artwork respond to each other.

(4) Now, using a computer, you can change three different kinds of art. (5) Movies, paintings, and photographs. (6) For example, using a graphics program, you can take your photo of a sleeping dog and change it any way you like. (7) Using the drawing tool, you could change its closed eyes to open ones. (8) You might even make the dog wink. (9) You can change the title of the artwork. (10) Let's say the first title you chose for this photo is "Dr Smith's Best Friend." (11) You can change the title by clicking on the text and typing in another. (12) Would you like to adjust the color of the dogs fur? (13) Simply locate the color tool. (14) Then click on the fur to change its color. (15) These are just a few examples of ways to rework still images. (16) Similar types of changes can be made to movies and portrits.

(17) Everyone should try interactive art. (18) You might share your art with your family. (19) Maybe they will be encouraged to experiment and be creative, too. (20) Remember that because the art remains interactive, your family might suggest new transformations!

Name _____ Date _____

Now answer Numbers 14 through 19 on your Answer Sheet. Base your answers on the changes Laura should make.

14 What change should be made in sentence 1?

    F. change *know* to **knew**

    G. insert a comma after *computer*

    H. change *your* to **you're**

    I. change *vision* to **vishun**

15 What is the best way to revise sentences 4 and 5?

    A. Now, using a computer, you can change three different (movies, paintings, and photographs) kinds of art.

    B. Now, using a computer, you can change three different kinds of art: movies, paintings, and photographs.

    C. Now, using a computer, you can change three different kinds of art. Such as movies, paintings, and photographs.

    D. Now, using a computer, you can change three different kinds of art that is these: movies, paintings, and photographs.

16 Which phrase could best be added to the beginning of sentence 9?

    F. In conclusion,

    G. For example,

    H. In addition,

    I. As a result,

17 What change should be made in sentence 10?

    A. change *Let's* to **Lets**

    B. change *this* to **these**

    C. insert a period after **Dr**

    D. delete the period after *Friend*

Name _____ Date _____

18 What change should be made in sentence 12?

F. change *Would* to **Could**

G. change *dogs* to **dog's**

H. insert **more** after *fur*

I. change the question mark to a period

19 What change should be made in sentence 16?

A. change *types* to **type**

B. change *can* to **will**

C. insert a comma after *movies*

D. change *portrits* to **portraits**

Read the introduction and the passage "Pickles for a Park" before answering Numbers 20 through 25.

Juan wrote this passage about a woman who wants to improve a neighborhood park. Read his passage and think about the changes he should make.

Pickles for a Park

(1) Miss Pike walked to the Emery St Park every afternoon. (2) When she was a youngster, it was a popular place for children to play. (3) These days it was deserted. (4) The place was a mess.

(5) One day, Miss Pike pondered what she could do to improve the condition of the park. (6) She did not have much money but she was determined to transform the park into a wonderful place once again.

(7) As Miss Pike sat thinking about her dilemma, she looked at all the vegetables in her garden. (8) Miss Pikes vegetables were always the best in the neighborhood. (9) Fresh food flowed from her garden into her kitchen throughout the summer (June through August) and well into the fall (September through November). (10) Miss Pike grew everything, and the cucumbers were especially plentiful this year. (11) Finally, inspiration struck—she'd make pickles from the cucumbers and sell them as a fundraiser for the park!

(12) In all her years of gardening, Miss Pike had never canned or pickled anything. (13) She needed to do research to find out how to pickle cucumbers. (14) She found it was surprisingly easy to follow the recipes, and she learned quickly. (15) She made four kinds of pickles dill, sweet, bread-and-butter, and hot-pepper.

Name _____ Date _____

(16) All of the people in the neighborhood loved the pickles and they

bought every single jar of the tasty treats. (17) With the neighborhood's help,

Miss Pike raised plenty of money to clean up the park, plant new flowers, and

purchase new playground equipment.

Now answer Numbers 20 through 25 on your Answer Sheet. Base your answers on the changes Juan should make.

20 What change should be made in sentence 1?

    F. change *walked* to **walk**

    G. change *Emery* to **emery**

    H. change *St* to **St.**

    I. change *every* to **very**

21 Which word or phrase could best be added to the beginning of sentence 3?

    A. However,

    B. As a result,

    C. Therefore,

    D. For instance,

22 Which sentence could best be added after sentence 4?

    F. There were several other parks in the city.

    G. When Miss Pike was little, she loved to ride the merry-go-round.

    H. Miss Pike knew a lot of the children who lived in the neighborhood.

    I. There was trash everywhere, and the slides and swings were worn out.

23 What change should be made in sentence 6?

    A. change *did not* to **did'nt**

    B. change *have* to **had**

    C. insert a comma after *money*

    D. change *wonderful* to **full of wonder**

24 What change should be made in sentence 8?

    F. insert **Because** at the beginning of the sentence

    G. change *Pikes* to **Pike's**

    H. change *were* to **was**

    I. insert a comma after *best*

25 What change should be made in sentence 15?

    A. change *made* to **makes**

    B. change *four* to **for**

    C. insert a colon after *pickles*

    D. delete the comma after *sweet*

Writing to Inform

Read the prompt and plan your response.

> Most people have an activity that they enjoy.
>
> Think about an activity that you enjoy.
>
> Now write an essay explaining what this activity is and why you enjoy it.

Planning Page

Use this space to make your notes before you begin writing. The writing on this page will NOT be scored.

_____

_____

_____

_____

_____

_____

_____

_____

_____

_____

_____

_____

_____

_____

Name _____ Date _____

Begin writing your response here. The writing on this page and the next page WILL be scored.

_____

_____

_____

_____

_____

_____

_____

_____

_____

_____

_____

_____

_____

_____

_____

_____

_____

_____

_____

_____

_____

_____

_____

_____

_____

_____

Name _____ Date _____

_____

_____

_____

_____

_____

_____

_____

_____

_____

_____

_____

_____

_____

_____

_____

_____

_____

_____

_____

_____

_____

_____

_____

Reading Complex Text

Read the play "Tortoise and the Birds: A West African Folktale." As you read, stop and answer each question. Use evidence from the play to support your answers.

Tortoise and the Birds: A West African Folktale

Cast of Characters:

Narrator

Tortoise

Parrot

Lark

Dove

Ibis

Cuckoo

Sparrow

Emperor of the Cloud People

Cloud People (crowd)

Scene 1

Narrator: Back in the times when animals could talk, Tortoise was ambling through the forest in search of food and water. Both were scarce since a drought had fallen over the land. Stomach rumbling, Tortoise plodded along, straining his neck high and low to see if he might spot mangoes in the trees or a puddle of groundwater. As Tortoise approached a clearing, he observed a company of birds. They were prattling excitedly and preening their colorful feathers.

Tortoise: [to himself] Those birds certainly don't sound like starving creatures, and those feathers are looking mighty healthy-looking. [smiling slyly] I must investigate this matter.

As Tortoise emerges into the clearing, the birds stop chattering and fall into hushed silence.

Tortoise: Greetings, my feathered friends. Might I ask the reason for your festive mood?

The birds exchange cautious glances. Finally, Parrot opens her beak.

Name _____ Date _____

Parrot: If you must know, for the past few days we have taken up the Cloud People's invitation to join their great feast in the sky. We decided not to share the invitation with you four-legged land dwellers, given that none of you have wings.

> **1** Why do the birds exchange cautious glances before responding to Tortoise?
>
> _____
>
> _____
>
> _____

Tortoise: It certainly does look like you have been dining well. Your feathers are shinier than I have ever seen.

Lark: Oh, if you could only see the delicious, mouth-watering spread the Cloud People put forth: yam dumplings, pineapples . . .

Tortoise: What if I told you that I could ensure that the Cloud People gave you only the richest, finest foods they have? If you helped me create a pair of wings so that I could go along, I could represent you as your spokesperson to the Cloud People.

While the birds consult one another, Tortoise tries to suppress a cunning grin.

Dove: All right, it's been decided. We have all agreed to pluck several of our own feathers. Out of those, we will fashion you your own set of wings.

Narrator: And so the birds busily set to work creating a set of wings with a hodgepodge of vibrant feathers. The birds presented this gift to Tortoise, who promptly donned the wings and paraded his newest feature all over the clearing to the amusement of all the birds. Then, with Tortoise flying rather awkwardly in tow, the troupe dispatched for the kingdom of the Cloud People.

Scene 2
Narrator: Hundreds of miles above the earth, the birds and Tortoise alighted on the edge of the Cloud People's kingdom where the Cloud People cordially received them.

Emperor of the Cloud People: Warmest welcomes to our land-dwelling friends! And who is this newest winged friend who boasts such a brilliant assortment of feathers?

Tortoise: [stepping forward] They call me "All-Of-You." I am the emperor of all land dwellers. [Tortoise bows deeply, spreading his feathers like a fan.]

Narrator: Tortoise's introduction baffled the birds, but it caused a great flurry of activity and excitement amongst the Cloud People, who were impressed with this ruler (however

Name _____ Date _____

strange-looking he might be) and his ornate feathers. They set about preparing a great feast in honor of the ruler of the land dwellers. When it was ready, they invited Tortoise and the birds to sit.

---

2   Why does Tortoise spread "his feathers like a fan"?

_____

_____

_____

Tortoise: For whom is all of this magnificent food?

Cloud People: [in unison] We have prepared this feast for ALL OF YOU! [The Cloud People gesture toward all of their guests.]

Tortoise: Many thanks to you! I am honored!

Narrator: And without hesitation, Tortoise dug into the fine food and drink before him, gobbling them down so fast that all the birds could manage to do was gape. The Cloud People, though curious about this unusual-seeming custom for the ruler to eat in place of his people, just shrugged; they were happy that they had pleased this "All-Of-You." Having devoured the food, Tortoise waved farewell to the Cloud People and launched his overstuffed body into the sky. Flustered, angry, and, of course, hungry, the birds followed him.

Scene 3

Ibis: [to the other birds] That deceitful Tortoise! He is not worthy to fly with our feathers!

Cuckoo: He must pay for his greed and his tricks. Come—let us seize our feathers back and leave him stranded on a cloud where he must find his own way back to the earth.

The birds surround Tortoise mid-flight and proceed to pluck the feathers from his wings. Clinging to a cloud, Tortoise calls out to Sparrow.

Tortoise: Oh, tiny Sparrow, do not leave me marooned up here! At the very least, won't you convince the other birds to build me a landing pad down below, made out of the softest things you can find? Please!

Sparrow: Well . . . [considering] I suppose. I will call to you when we are finished.

Sparrow flies towards earth, leaving a very relieved-looking Tortoise suspended on a cloud.

<u>Scene 4</u>

Narrator: Back on the earth, Sparrow motions for all of the birds to gather around. Tortoise is not the only trickster amongst them. Sparrow, too, has a trick up his sleeve.

Sparrow: Go and collect all of the hardest things that you can find and pile them here in this clearing. We are going to teach that Tortoise a lesson he will never forget!

The birds disperse, returning after awhile with their mouths full of rocks, sticks, and clumps of earth. When the pile is high, Sparrow scans the clouds above for Tortoise's figure.

Sparrow: Tortoise, you may let go now. The pile is ready!

---

3 As a result of the narrator's role in the play, what information is known to the audience but NOT to Tortoise?

_____

_____

_____

Narrator: And so Tortoise did just that. He let go and plummeted to the earth where he landed with a hard thud on the unforgiving pile, breaking his precious shell into a hundred pieces. Otherwise unharmed, Tortoise collected the pieces of his shell and with a loud "harrumph" marched off into the forest. To this day, Tortoise sports a shell that appears patched together, rather than his once-sleek, blemish-free shell.

Tortoise: [walking away and gritting his teeth] Scarred shell or not, those birds have yet to see the last of my mischief. . . .

---

4 How do the ideas in this play support the advice that "honesty is the best policy"? Explain why Tortoise should have followed this advice.

_____

_____

_____

_____

_____

Name _____ Date _____

Skunk Scout

Answer Numbers 1 through 10 on your Answer Sheet. Base your answers on the novel *Skunk Scout.*

1 Teddy is upset when his father tells him that he will give Teddy the fish store when he grows up, because

    A. Teddy dislikes fish.

    B. his father's hands always smell.

    C. Bobby is the one who deserves the fish store.

    D. Teddy is not sure he is ready to decide what his future will be.

2 Teddy plays the "only child game" because

    F. it is a fun game.

    G. he dislikes his brother.

    H. he wants to annoy his brother.

    I. he has mixed feelings about having a brother.

3 Teddy tries to learn about the outdoors from one of Bobby's books because he

    A. is curious.

    B. is preparing himself for camping.

    C. wants to impress Bobby and Uncle Curtis.

    D. wants to convince his grandmother that camping is safe.

4 On the way to the camping place, why does Uncle Curtis keep losing his way?

    F. He gets distracted easily.

    G. The boys tell him to go in the wrong direction.

    H. He is testing the boys to see if they know their way.

    I. He wants the boys to tell Grandmother that they got lost.

Name _____ Date _____

5 Who is best at finding the way when the group is lost?

    A. Bobby

    B. Curtis

    C. Grandmother

    D. Teddy

6 What "big as a mountain" mistake does Teddy make that prevents the group from eating good meals?

    F. He brings candy with him.

    G. He puts the food in an ice chest with dry ice.

    H. He brings marshmallows that attract a raccoon.

    I. He forgets the ice chest at home with all of the food in it.

7 What does Teddy discover about Uncle Curtis that changes how Teddy feels about him?

    A. Uncle Curtis is a lot like Teddy.

    B. Uncle Curtis is his father's brother.

    C. Uncle Curtis wants to go home, too.

    D. Uncle Curtis likes Teddy better than he likes Bobby.

8 Teddy begins to enjoy the hike when he

    F. sees a bear.

    G. finds the way back.

    H. notices the sights and smells of nature.

    I. has a long talk with Uncle Curtis about not wanting to own a fish store.

Name _____ Date _____

9 The most fascinating thing that Teddy saw on the trip was the

    A. skunk.

    B. raccoon.

    C. television antennas.

    D. courtship of the snakes.

10 Where did Lawrence Yep get his ideas for the camping adventures in *Skunk Scout*?

    F. *Skunk Scout* is an autobiography.

    G. The stories in *Skunk Scout* are from Yep's imagination.

    H. *Skunk Scout* is based only on things that actually happened to Yep.

    I. *Skunk Scout* is based on things that happened to Yep and to people he knows.

Name _____ Date _____

Frindle

Answer Numbers 1 through 10 on your Answer Sheet. Base your answers on the novel *Frindle*.

1 The main purpose of the illustration on page 30 is to show that

    A. dogs come in many varieties.

    B. dogs are important in this story.

    C. Mrs. Granger knows a lot about dogs.

    D. there are many different words for "dog."

2 Which of the following statements best defines Nick's character?

    F. Nick is bossy.

    G. Nick is stubborn.

    H. Nick is determined.

    I. Nick is a troublemaker.

3 What event leads Nick to invent the word *frindle*?

    A. He buys a pen at a store.

    B. He finds a pen on the street.

    C. He returns Janet's gold pen.

    D. He remembers saying *frindle* as a child.

4 The oath Nick's classmates take to say *frindle* supports the idea that

    F. Nick makes the rules.

    G. it's important to keep a promise.

    H. students should decide what they learn.

    I. words will spread if enough people use them.

5 Mrs. Granger punishes the students for saying *frindle* because she thinks

    A. opposing the word will stop its use.

    B. the students are being disrespectful.

    C. the students should follow the rules.

    D. opposing the word will help spread its use.

6 Which of the following statements from the novel is a fact?

    F. "The dictionary is the finest tool ever made for educating young minds."

    G. "All the words in the dictionary were made up by people."

    H. "She's really a very fine teacher."

    I. "As the boy's guardian, you need to do the right thing about all this."

7 What conclusion can the reader draw about Mrs. Granger from the letter she has Nick sign?

    A. She is mysterious.

    B. She wants Nick to fail with his word.

    C. She likes to keep records of everything.

    D. She wants Nick to succeed with his word.

8 What conclusion can the reader draw from the news broadcast about *frindle*?

    F. The news media makes Nick famous.

    G. TV is more important than newspapers.

    H. The news media causes people to argue.

    I. The news media spreads ideas to lots of people.

Name _____ Date _____

9 Which conclusion is supported by the illustration on page 103?

    A. Nick hates to study.

    B. Nick still likes baseball.

    C. Nick prefers a pen to a computer.

    D. Nick doesn't remember Mrs. Granger.

10 In the end, Nick "wins" because

    F. he becomes rich.

    G. Mrs. Granger gives up.

    H. he does well in college.

    I. *frindle* is listed in the dictionary.

Name _____ Date _____

Mysteries of the Mummy Kids

Answer Numbers 1 through 10 on your Answer Sheet. Base your answers on the novel *Mysteries of the Mummy Kids*.

1 What is the author's purpose in writing *Mysteries of the Mummy Kids*?

   A. to entertain

   B. to inform readers about King Tut

   C. to inform readers about mummies

   D. to persuade readers to study historical cultures

2 Experts know that Tut was a king because

   F. of stories told by the Egyptians.

   G. he was buried with the objects of a king.

   H. there were pictures on the walls of other tombs.

   I. the location of his tomb was where a king's tomb would be.

3 According to the book, where has the oldest mummy been discovered?

   A. in the Valley of the Kings

   B. near Chile's Camarones Valley

   C. in the remote town of Urumchi

   D. near the province of Drenthe, Holland

4 Which of the following sentences from the novel states an opinion?

   F. "Five hundred years ago, nearly ten million Incan people lived in Tahuantinsuyu, the Land of Four Quarters."

   G. "He finally opened the pharaoh's tomb on February 17, 1923."

   H. "Deep pockets of oxygen-starved rainwater rested between mounds of surface soil."

   I. "We find ourselves nearly hypnotized by mummies because we all crave meaningful human connections."

5 What does the map on page 6 help the reader understand?

A. the locations of Incan mummies

B. the dates and location of the Inca Empire

C. the names of all of the world's oceans

D. the distance from North America to South America

6 Which of the following sentences from the novel states a fact?

F. "Somehow it just didn't seem right to put this person's picture on a postcard without telling me something about him."

G. "No matter where they rest, these mummies, including Tutankhamun, have a glorious history in common."

H. "The perfect mix of science and technology made Sherit big news."

I. "The mummies of Urumchi were found in China, so it was originally believed they were of Chinese descent."

7 Civilization's oldest mummies were found in

A. Chile.

B. Egypt.

C. Greenland.

D. Sicily.

8 To learn more about the Incan mummies, the reader would look in the chapter titled

F. South American Mysteries.

G. Mysterious Mummies of Egypt.

H. Kid Mummies of Europe and Asia.

I. Kid Mummy Mysteries from North America.

Name _____ Date _____

9 The mummies of northwestern Europe's bog people were preserved by

A. peat.

B. water.

C. chemicals.

D. freezing temperatures.

10 What does the author suggest about the future of mummification?

F. It has no future.

G. It will definitely be common practice.

H. It is possible that it will be common practice.

I. It is illegal and could never happen in the future.